Endpapers: An aerial view of rice paddies in the New Territories,
Hong Kong.

Kingfisher Books, Grisewood & Dempsey Ltd,
Elsley House, 24–30 Great Titchfield Street,
London W1P 7AD

This revised and expanded edition published in 1987
by Kingfisher Books.
Reprinted 1987, 1988, 1989 (twice), 1990, 1991 (twice)
First published as *First Picture Atlas* in 1980.
Copyright © Kingfisher Books Ltd 1980, 1987

BRITISH LIBRARY CATALOGUING IN PUBLICATION DATA

The Kingfisher children's world atlas.
  1. Atlases —— Juvenile literature.
  I. Olliver, Jane
  912   G1021

ISBN 0–86272–239–X

Assistant Editor: Nan Froman
Designed by the Pinpoint Design Company
Maps drawn by Product (Graphics) Support Limited
Typeset by Waveney Typesetters, Norwich, England
Printed in Italy by Vallardi Industrie Grafiche, Milan

THE KINGFISHER

CHILDREN'S
WORLD
ATLAS

EDITED BY JANE OLLIVER

Kingfisher Books

Contents

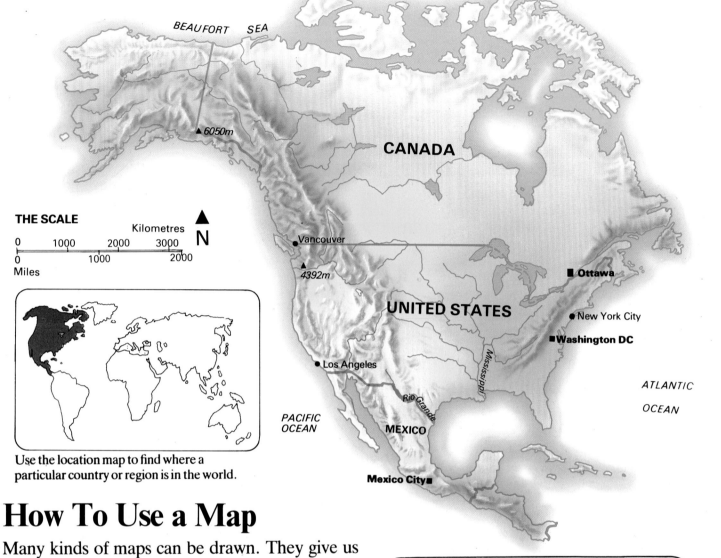

BEAUFORT SEA

CANADA

▲ 6050m

THE SCALE

Kilometres

▲
N

Vancouver ●

▲ 4392m

■ **Ottawa**

UNITED STATES

● New York City

■**Washington DC**

● Los Angeles

Mississippi

ATLANTIC OCEAN

PACIFIC OCEAN

Rio Grande

MEXICO

Mexico City■

Use the location map to find where a particular country or region is in the world.

How To Use a Map

Many kinds of maps can be drawn. They give us different information. A *political* map, like the one on pages 10–11, shows the boundaries of the world's countries. The physical map on pages 12–13 shows the land's surface with its oceans, rivers, lakes and mountains. Colours and *symbols* are used on maps to give information. Look at the map above. To see what the colours and symbols mean, check the *key* on the right.

Maps are much smaller than the actual area of the countries they show. But they are always drawn to *scale*. Scale means the comparison between the map size and the real size. If the scale is written like this – 1:800,000, it means that one centimetre on the map stands for 800,000 centimetres (8 kilometres) on the ground. The maps in this atlas have a bar scale. You can measure any distance on the map, then compare it to the bar scale to find the real land distance.

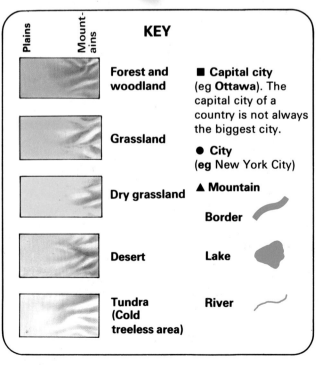

Plains

Mountains

KEY

Forest and woodland

Grassland

Dry grassland

Desert

Tundra (Cold treeless area)

■ **Capital city** (eg **Ottawa**). The capital city of a country is not always the biggest city.

● **City** (eg New York City)

▲ **Mountain**

Border

Lake

River

Maps and Mapmaking

Our Earth is one of nine planets circling around the Sun. It is the fifth largest planet in the Solar System. The Earth is shaped like a ball. But it is slightly flattened at the top and bottom.

We can show the Earth's land and seas as they are by drawing a map on the surface of a *globe*. A globe is a round ball, shaped like the Earth. You can see a picture of a globe on the right. When it turns, we can see all the sides one by one. Look at these four views of the same globe.

▲ A globe

Western **Eastern** **Northern** **Southern**

But if we want to show all the Earth's sides at once on flat paper, we have to draw a *projection*. A projection is a flat drawing of rounded sections of the globe. It is impossible to lay a curved surface flat without twisting and pulling some of the sections. Try drawing a picture on an orange. Then peel the orange in segments and flatten them on a table. You will not be able to do it without squashing the peel out of shape, or *distorting* it. What has happened to your drawing? It is distorted. All maps of the world are distorted in one way or another.

The surface of the globe being peeled off.

The surface of the globe stretched flat.

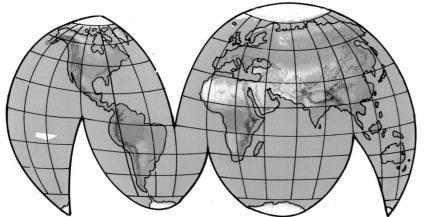

Above and left you can see one method of peeling the surface off a globe to make a flat map. The lines on the map running from north to south are lines of *longitude*. The lines running from east to west are the lines of *latitude*. These lines are very useful. Map-makers use them to make sure that cities and boundaries are put in the right place on the map.

The Earth:
Facts and Figures

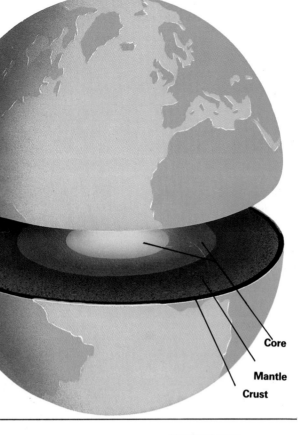

Core

Mantle

Crust

EARTH FACTS

Circumference round the Equator: 40,075 kilometres.

Circumference round the Poles: 40,007 kilometres.

Distance to centre of Earth: about 6370 kilometres.

Surface area: about 510,065,600 square kilometres; sea covers 71% of the surface of the Earth.

Average distance from the Sun: 149,600,000 kilometres; the Earth is further away from the Sun in July than in January.

Rotation Speed: at the Equator, the Earth rotates on its axis at 1660 kilometres per hour.

Speed in orbit: The Earth travels at 29·8 kilometres per second.

Average distance from Moon: 385,000 kilometres.

HIGHEST MOUNTAINS

	metres
Everest (Himalaya-Nepal/Tibet)	8863
Godwin Austen (Pakistan/India)	8607
Kanchenjunga (Himalaya-Nepal/Sikkim)	8597
Makalu (Himalaya-Nepal/Tibet)	8470
Dhaulagiri (Himalaya-Nepal)	8172
Nanga Parbat (Himalaya-India)	8126
Annapurna (Himalaya-Nepal)	8075
Communism Peak (Pamir-USSR)	7495
Aconcagua (Andes-Argentina)	6960
McKinley (Alaska-USA)	6194
Kilimanjaro (Tanzania)	5895

LONGEST RIVERS

	kilometres
Nile (Africa)	6670
Amazon (S. America)	6437
Mississippi-Missouri-Red Rock (N. America)	6231
Yenisei (USSR)	5540
Yangtze (China)	5470
Ob-Irtysh (USSR)	5150
Zaire* (Africa)	4828
Lena (USSR)	4828
Amur (Asia)	4506
Hwang Ho (China)	4345
Mackenzie-Peace (Canada)	4240
Mekong (SE. Asia)	4184

*Formerly Congo River

LARGEST ISLANDS

	square kilometres
Greenland	2,175,600
New Guinea	794,090
Borneo	751,078
Madagascar	587,041
Baffin I.	476,066
Sumatra	431,982
Honshu	230,822
Great Britain	229,522
Ellesmere	198,393
Victoria I.	192,695

OCEANS

	square kilometres
Pacific	181,000,000
Atlantic	106,000,000
Indian	73,490,000
Arctic	14,350,000

LARGEST LAKES

	square kilometres
Caspian Sea (USSR/Iran)	438,695
Superior (USA/Canada)	82,409
Victoria Nyanza (Africa)	69,484
Aral (USSR)	67,770
Huron (USA/Canada)	59,570
Michigan (USA)	58,016
Baikal (USSR)	34,180
Tanganyika (Africa)	31,999
Great Bear (Canada)	31,598
Malawi* (Africa)	28,490

*Also called Lake Nyasa

The highest waterfall is part of the Angel Falls, Venezuela.

MAJOR WATERFALLS

Highest	metres
Angel Falls (Venezuela)	979
Tugela Falls (South Africa)	948
Yosemite Falls (California)	739

Greatest volume	cubic metres per second
Niagara (N. America)	6,000

DESERTS

	square kilometres
Sahara	8,400,000
Australian Desert	1,550,000
Arabian Desert	1,300,000
Gobi	1,040,000
Kalahari	520,000

The highest mountain is the peak of Everest above Khumbu glacier.

The largest desert is the Sahara which stretches across northern Africa.

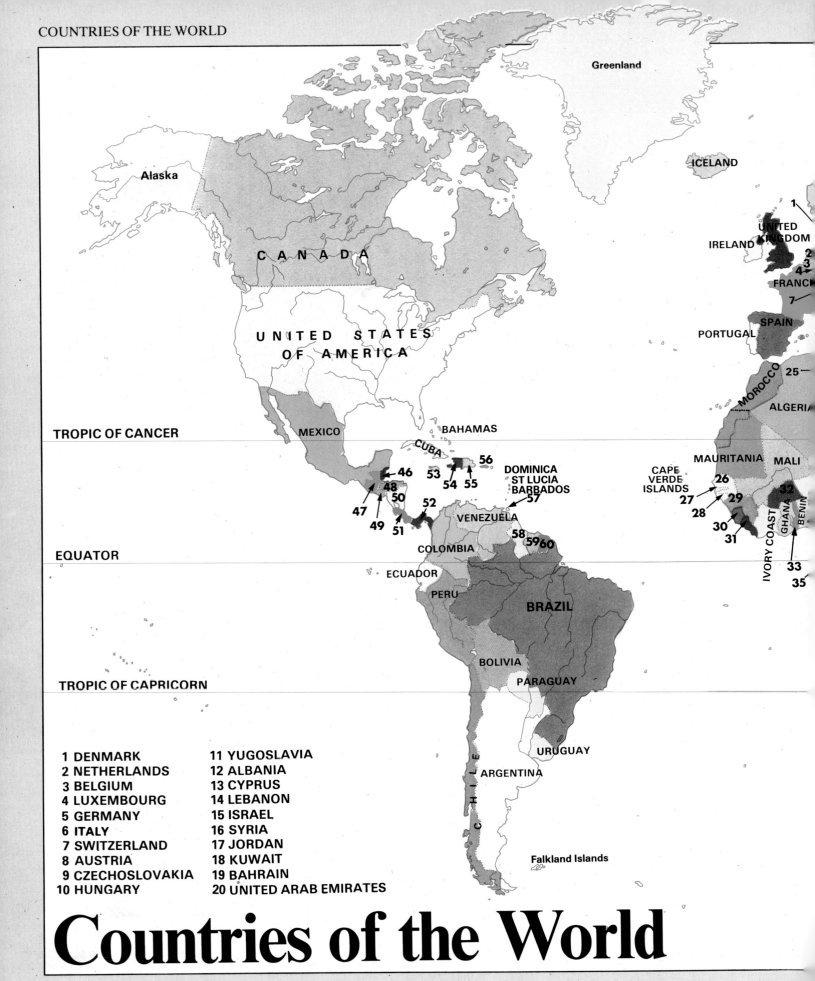

Greenland

Alaska

ICELAND

1

UNITED
KINGDOM

IRELAND

2
3
4

FRANCE

7

SPAIN

PORTUGAL

C A N A D A

U N I T E D   S T A T E S
O F   A M E R I C A

25

MOROCCO

ALGERIA

TROPIC OF CANCER

MEXICO

BAHAMAS

MAURITANIA

MALI

CUBA

56

CAPE
VERDE
ISLANDS

46

53

DOMINICA
ST LUCIA
BARBADOS

26

32

54 55

27

29

48
50

57

28

GHANA

BENIN

47

52

VENEZUELA

30

49

51

58

31

IVORY COAST

EQUATOR

COLOMBIA

59 60

33

ECUADOR

35

PERU

BRAZIL

BOLIVIA

TROPIC OF CAPRICORN

PARAGUAY

URUGUAY

C H I L E

ARGENTINA

Falkland Islands

1 DENMARK	11 YUGOSLAVIA
2 NETHERLANDS	12 ALBANIA
3 BELGIUM	13 CYPRUS
4 LUXEMBOURG	14 LEBANON
5 GERMANY	15 ISRAEL
6 ITALY	16 SYRIA
7 SWITZERLAND	17 JORDAN
8 AUSTRIA	18 KUWAIT
9 CZECHOSLOVAKIA	19 BAHRAIN
10 HUNGARY	20 UNITED ARAB EMIRATES

Countries of the World

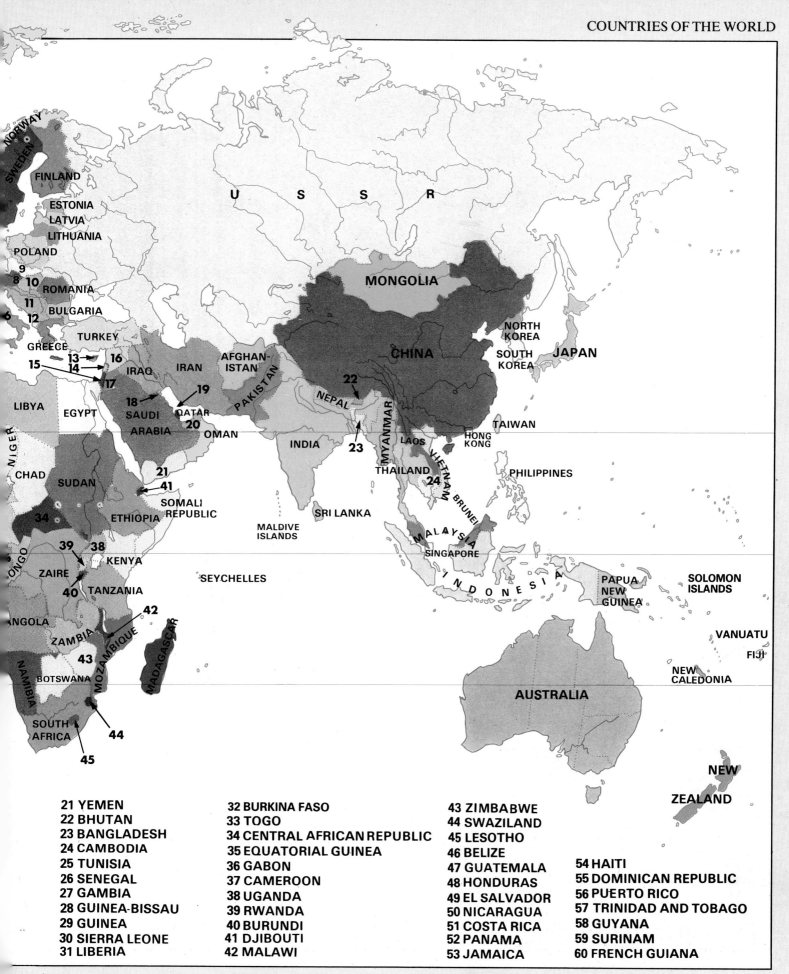

NORWAY
SWEDEN
FINLAND
ESTONIA
LATVIA
LITHUANIA
POLAND
9
8 10 ROMANIA
11
6 12 BULGARIA
GREECE
TURKEY
13 → 16
15
14 →
17
LIBYA
EGYPT
IRAQ
IRAN
AFGHAN-ISTAN
PAKISTAN
18 →
19
SAUDI ARABIA
QATAR
20
OMAN
NEPAL
NIGER
CHAD
SUDAN
21
41
SOMALI REPUBLIC
34
ETHIOPIA
39 38
ONGO
ZAIRE
KENYA
40
TANZANIA
42
ANGOLA
ZAMBIA
43
MOZAMBIQUE
MADAGASCAR
BOTSWANA
NAMIBIA
SOUTH AFRICA
44
45

U S S R

MONGOLIA

CHINA

NORTH KOREA
SOUTH KOREA
JAPAN

TAIWAN

HONG KONG

22

INDIA

23
MYANMAR
LAOS
THAILAND
VIETNAM
BRUNEI
24

SRI LANKA

MALDIVE ISLANDS

SEYCHELLES

MALAYSIA
SINGAPORE
INDONESIA

PHILIPPINES

PAPUA NEW GUINEA

SOLOMON ISLANDS

VANUATU
FIJI

NEW CALEDONIA

AUSTRALIA

NEW ZEALAND

21 YEMEN
22 BHUTAN
23 BANGLADESH
24 CAMBODIA
25 TUNISIA
26 SENEGAL
27 GAMBIA
28 GUINEA-BISSAU
29 GUINEA
30 SIERRA LEONE
31 LIBERIA

32 BURKINA FASO
33 TOGO
34 CENTRAL AFRICAN REPUBLIC
35 EQUATORIAL GUINEA
36 GABON
37 CAMEROON
38 UGANDA
39 RWANDA
40 BURUNDI
41 DJIBOUTI
42 MALAWI

43 ZIMBABWE
44 SWAZILAND
45 LESOTHO
46 BELIZE
47 GUATEMALA
48 HONDURAS
49 EL SALVADOR
50 NICARAGUA
51 COSTA RICA
52 PANAMA
53 JAMAICA

54 HAITI
55 DOMINICAN REPUBLIC
56 PUERTO RICO
57 TRINIDAD AND TOBAGO
58 GUYANA
59 SURINAM
60 FRENCH GUIANA

The Continents

A R C

NORTH

AMERICA

P A C I F I C   O C E A N

ATLANTIC OCEAN

TROPIC OF CANCER

EQUATOR

SOUTH

AMERICA   **TROPIC OF CAPRICORN**

A N T A R C

FACTS ABOUT EUROPE
(including all the USSR)

Area: Europe apart from USSR and the Baltics is 4,874,040 square kilometres. USSR and the Baltics are 22,402,000 square kilometres.

Population: Europe, about 492,000,000; USSR and the Baltics, about 278,000,000.

Number of countries: 36

Largest country: The USSR which is in Europe and Asia.

Smallest country: Vatican City

Highest mountain: Communism Peak in the Pamir Mountains in USSR, 7495 metres. Mount Elbruz in the Caucasus Mountains in USSR, 5633 metres.

Largest lake: The Caspian Sea, 438,695 square kilometres.

Longest rivers: The Yenisei River, USSR is 5540 kilometres, the Ob-Irtysh is 5150 kilometres and the Volga is 2293 kilometres. The Danube flows from Germany to the Black Sea. It is 1700 kilometres.

FACTS ABOUT NORTH & CENTRAL AMERICA

Area: 24,249,000 square kilometres including North and Central America, the West Indies and Greenland.

Population: About 400,000,000 people.

Number of countries: 22

Largest country: Canada

Smallest country: St. Kitts and Nevis

Highest mountain: Mount McKinley in Alaska, 6194 metres.

Largest lake: Lake Superior, 82,409 square kilometres.

Longest rivers: Mississippi-Missouri-Red Rock (USA) 6231 kilometres; Mackenzie-Peace (Canada) 4240 kilometres.

FACTS ABOUT SOUTH AMERICA

Area: 17,600,000 square kilometres.

Population: About 271,076,000 people.

Number of countries: 13

Largest country: Brazil

Smallest country: French Guiana

Highest mountain: Mount Aconcagua in Argentina is 6960 metres high.

Largest lake: Lake Titicaca in Bolivia and Peru, 8300 square kilometres.

Longest river: The River Amazon is 6437 kilometres.

FACTS ABOUT AFRICA

Area: 30,319,000 square kilometres.

Population: About 550,500,000 people.

Number of countries: 53

Largest country: Sudan

Smallest country: Seychelles

Highest mountain: Mt Kilimanjaro in Tanzania is 5895 metres high.

Largest lake: Lake Victoria in Kenya, Tanzania, and Uganda covers 69,484 square kilometres.

Longest rivers: The River Nile is 6670 kilometres long. It is the longest river in the world. The Zaire is 4828 kilometres, and the Niger 4000 kilometres.

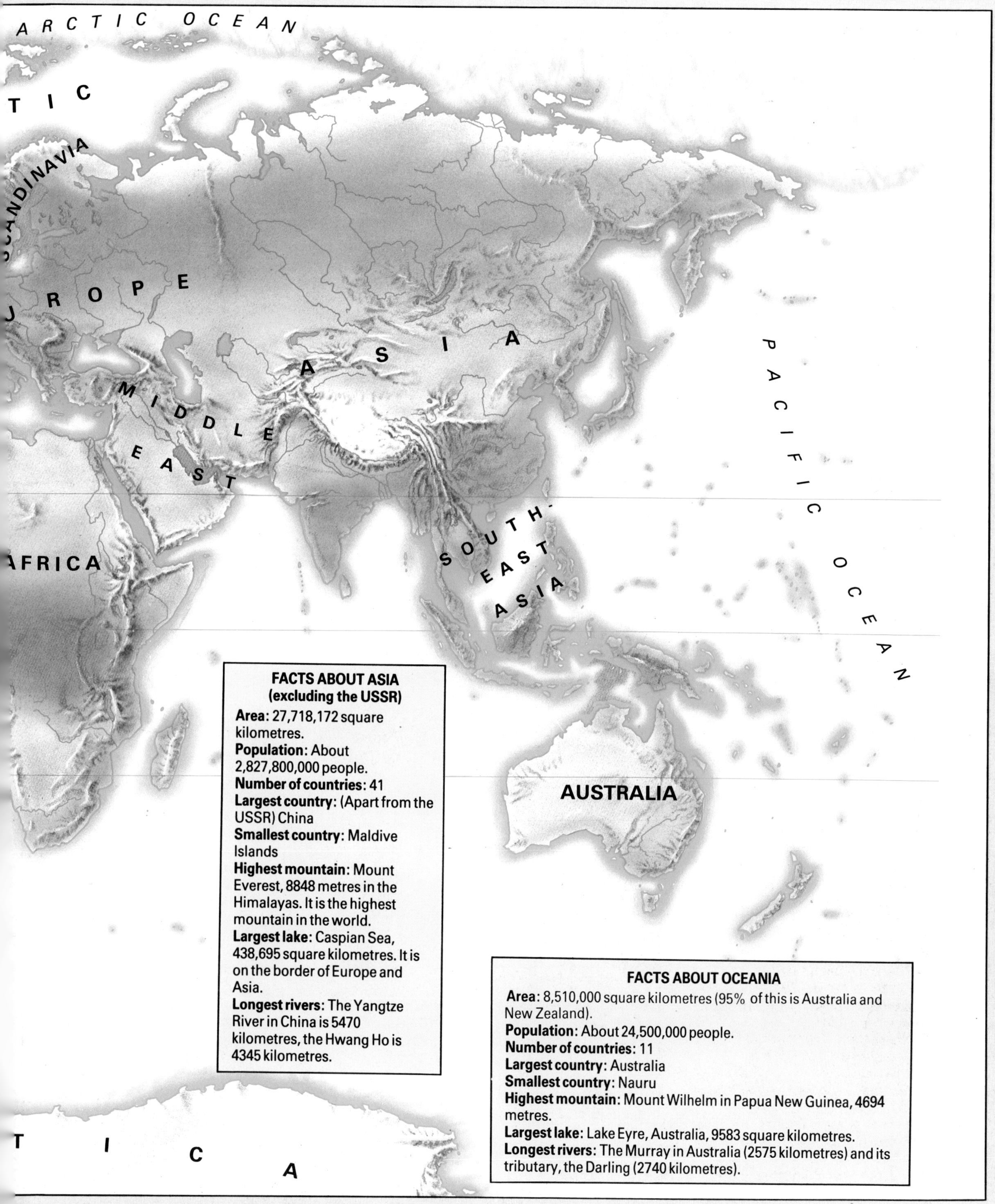

ARCTIC OCEAN

SCANDINAVIA

EUROPE

ASIA

MIDDLE EAST

PACIFIC OCEAN

AFRICA

SOUTH-EAST ASIA

AUSTRALIA

FACTS ABOUT ASIA
(excluding the USSR)
Area: 27,718,172 square kilometres.
Population: About 2,827,800,000 people.
Number of countries: 41
Largest country: (Apart from the USSR) China
Smallest country: Maldive Islands
Highest mountain: Mount Everest, 8848 metres in the Himalayas. It is the highest mountain in the world.
Largest lake: Caspian Sea, 438,695 square kilometres. It is on the border of Europe and Asia.
Longest rivers: The Yangtze River in China is 5470 kilometres, the Hwang Ho is 4345 kilometres.

FACTS ABOUT OCEANIA
Area: 8,510,000 square kilometres (95% of this is Australia and New Zealand).
Population: About 24,500,000 people.
Number of countries: 11
Largest country: Australia
Smallest country: Nauru
Highest mountain: Mount Wilhelm in Papua New Guinea, 4694 metres.
Largest lake: Lake Eyre, Australia, 9583 square kilometres.
Longest rivers: The Murray in Australia (2575 kilometres) and its tributary, the Darling (2740 kilometres).

TICA

Scandinavia and Finland

Thousands of years ago, Scandinavia was covered with ice sheets and glaciers. These cut deep *fiords* into the coastline and formed many lakes and islands. Iceland is the most northern country in Europe. It still has many snowfields. It is also dotted with many hot springs, steaming geysers and over 100 volcanoes.

Most Scandinavians enjoy a high standard of living. Sweden is the largest and richest of the countries. Over half the Swedish people live in modern cities, such as Stockholm and Goteborg. Many earn their living by manufacturing paper and other wood products. Sweden, Norway and Finland have large areas of forest.

Scandinavia's coastal waters teem with fish. Fishermen, mainly from Iceland and Norway, catch large quantities of cod and herring which are canned or frozen in fish-processing factories.

Dairy farming is important in Denmark. Only one-fifth of the people are farmers, but they use the latest machinery and farming methods.

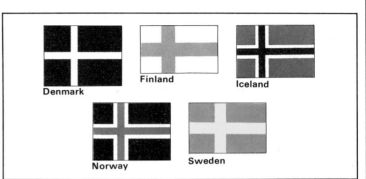

Denmark Finland Iceland

Norway Sweden

Above: The Copenhagen waterfront is very busy. Fishing, shipping and tourism are important industries in Denmark.

Left: There are hundreds of fiords in Norway. The force of the water falling down cliffs is used to make electricity.

Right: The sculpture in Copenhagen Harbour is called the Little Mermaid after the fairy tale by Hans Christian Andersen.

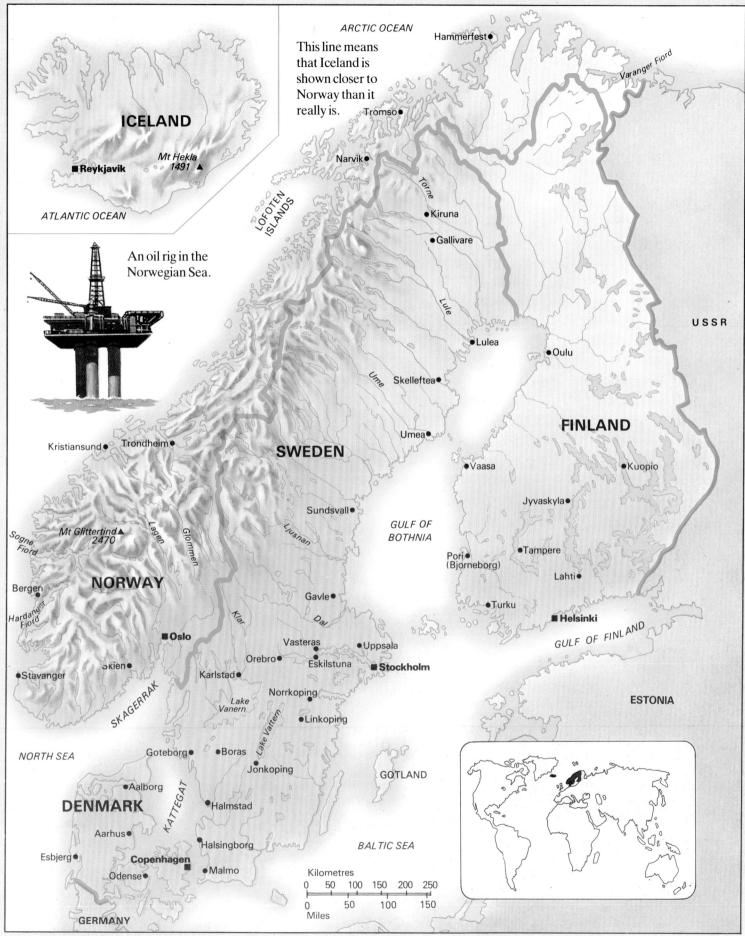

ICELAND

■ **Reykjavik**

Mt Hekla
1491 ▲

ATLANTIC OCEAN

This line means
that Iceland is
shown closer to
Norway than it
really is.

An oil rig in the
Norwegian Sea.

ARCTIC OCEAN   Hammerfest

Varanger Fiord

Tromso

Narvik

*LOFOTEN
ISLANDS*

Kiruna

Gallivare

Torne

Lule

Lulea

Oulu

USSR

Skelleftea

Ume

Umea

FINLAND

Kristiansund   Trondheim

SWEDEN

Vaasa

Kuopio

Jyvaskyla

Mt Glittertind ▲
2470

Lagen

Glommen

Sundsvall

Ljusnan

*GULF OF
BOTHNIA*

Tampere

Pori
(Bjorneborg)

Lahti

*Sogne
Fiord*

Bergen

NORWAY

*Hardanger
Fiord*

Klar

Gavle

Dal

Turku

■ **Helsinki**

Skien

■ **Oslo**

Stavanger

Vasteras

Orebro

Eskilstuna

Uppsala

Stockholm

GULF OF FINLAND

Karlstad

Norrkoping

*Lake
Vanern*

Linkoping

Lake Vattern

ESTONIA

NORTH SEA

Goteborg

Boras

Jonkoping

GOTLAND

Aalborg

KATTEGAT

DENMARK

Halmstad

Aarhus

Halsingborg

BALTIC SEA

Esbjerg

Copenhagen

Malmo

Odense

Kilometres

0 50 100 150 200 250

0   50   100   150
Miles

SKAGERRAK

GERMANY

Netherlands, Belgium and Luxembourg

Netherlands   **Belgium**   **Luxembourg**

The Netherlands, Belgium and Luxembourg are known as the Low Countries because much of the land is flat and below sea-level. In the Netherlands high *dykes*, or sea walls, have been built around low-lying lands, which are called *polders*. Nearly a quarter of the Netherlands's land has been *reclaimed*, or taken back, from the sea in this way.

The Low Countries have a combined population of nearly 25 million. This makes them the most densely populated group of countries in Europe. They are also wealthy countries. Most people work in offices and factories, often in textile and electrical companies. Others work on the land. The farms are small and very modern. Dutch farmers grow either flowers or vegetables or keep cows. There are also large iron and steel mills in Belgium and Luxembourg. Luxembourgers are *bi-lingual*. They speak two languages – French and Luxemburgish.

Below left: A flower market and many beautiful old buildings can be found in the Grand Place of Brussels. Brussels is the headquarters of the Common Market (EEC).

Below: Windmills are often seen in the Dutch countryside. They were once used to pump water from polders to stop flooding.

Cheeses like Edam and Gouda are made in the Netherlands. They are sold in cheese markets.

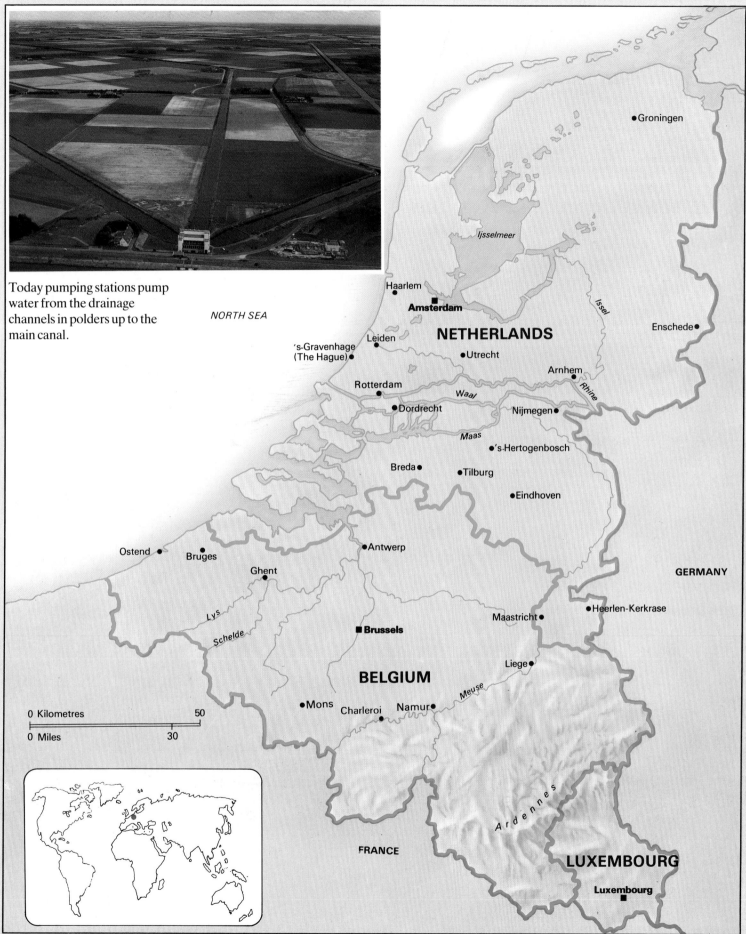

Today pumping stations pump water from the drainage channels in polders up to the main canal.

NORTH SEA

Groningen

Ijsselmeer

Issel

Enschede

Haarlem

Amsterdam

NETHERLANDS

Leiden

's-Gravenhage (The Hague)

Utrecht

Arnhem

Rhine

Rotterdam

Waal

Dordrecht

Nijmegen

Maas

's-Hertogenbosch

Breda

Tilburg

Eindhoven

Antwerp

Ostend

Bruges

Ghent

Lys

Schelde

■ **Brussels**

Maastricht

Heerlen-Kerkrase

GERMANY

Liege

BELGIUM

Meuse

Mons

Charleroi

Namur

0 Kilometres 50

0 Miles 30

FRANCE

Ardennes

LUXEMBOURG

Luxembourg ■

The British Isles

The British Isles is made up of two countries: the United Kingdom and the Republic of Ireland. The United Kingdom consists of Great Britain (England, Wales and Scotland) and Northern Ireland. Many people call the United Kingdom simply Britain. The Republic of Ireland or Eire was once part of the United Kingdom. But in 1921 it became a separate country.

A moist climate makes Britain and the Republic of Ireland ideal for farming. But in Britain one-third of the food must still be *imported*, or bought from other countries. The farms are too small to feed the large population.

Industry is very important in Britain. For every one person working on the land, there are ten people living and working in cities. Britain pays for the food it imports by selling manufactured products, such as cars, to other countries.

Britain is divided into many different districts with their own customs and *dialects*, or ways of speaking. In Wales children learn Welsh as well as English in schools.

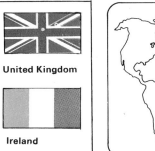

United Kingdom

Ireland

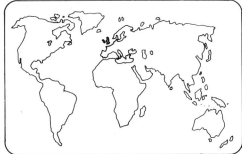

Above: The Houses of Parliament stand beside the River Thames in London. London is the capital of the United Kingdom.

Left: Fishguard is on the coast of South Wales. Most Welsh people live in cities in the south because the north is mountainous.

Below: Eilean Donan Castle is in north-west Scotland.

ORKNEY
ISLANDS

*John o'
Groats*

SHETLAND ISLANDS

A Scottish trawler

An oil-rig explores the
British oil field in the
North Sea.

HEBRIDES

North West Highlands

•Inverness
Loch Ness   *Dee*

•Aberdeen

▲*Ben Nevis*
1347m   *Grampians*

Tay

Oban•   •Dundee
       SCOTLAND •Perth

*Loch
Lomond*

•Dunfermline

Glasgow•
        Edinburgh
Clyde

•Ayr

•Londonderry

**NORTHERN
IRELAND**
                •Sligo
        Belfast

Tyne

•Newcastle
        •Sunderland
Eden •Middlesbrough
Lake   and Teesside
District

*N O R T H
S E A*

Pennines

ISLE OF MAN

*Lough
Mask*

Central Plains
•Galway

Dublin ■

*I R I S H
S E A*

Blackpool• •Bradford •Leeds
                                •York
           •Liverpool Manchester•   •Hull

▲*Snowdon*
1086m

•Sheffield
Trent

Shannon *Lough
Derg*

•Limerick

**REPUBLIC OF
IRELAND (EIRE)**

Barrow

*Wicklow
Mts*

Nottingham•
•Stoke-on-Trent
  •Wolverhampton   *The
Dudley•   •Walsall   Fens*
  Birmingham• •Leicester   •Great
        Cambrian Mts   Norwich• Yarmouth
                         Ouse
                •Coventry   •Cambridge
        Severn •Bedford
Avon   **ENGLAND**   •Ipswich

Waterford•
*Mts of
Kerry*

•Cork

•Fishguard

WALES

Oxford• *Chiltern Hills*
Cotswolds   *Thames* **London** ■

*A T L A N T I C

O C E A N*

•Swansea

Cardiff
       Bristol•
       •Bath

North Downs •Canterbury
                    •Dover

Exmoor

Exeter•
Dartmoor

•Plymouth

Southampton• •Portsmouth
Bournemouth•   •Brighton
        Isle of Wight •Eastbourne

Kilometres
0 20 40 60 80 100

0   25   50
Miles

ISLES OF
SCILLY

*Land's
End*

E N G L I S H   C H A N N E L

FRANCE

CHANNEL ISLANDS

France

France is the largest country in Europe, except for the USSR. Along most of its borders there are mountain ranges. The Jura Mountains separate France from Switzerland, the Pyrenees separate it from Spain, and the Vosges separate France partly from Germany. The Alps border France with Italy and contain Mont Blanc, which is the highest peak in France.

Although many French people work in factories, farming is very important. The warm climate and rich soil help farmers to grow cereals, fruit and sugar-beet. Grapes, used for making wine, are grown in most regions. But the main grapevine growing areas are in Bordeaux, Burgundy and Champagne. Dairy farming is also important and over 300 different cheeses are made.

Paris, Lyon and Marseille are the main cities in France. Painters and writers from all over the world have lived in Paris. Many tourists go there today to see its historic buildings, which include the Louvre, the Notre Dame Cathedral and the Eiffel Tower.

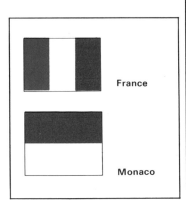

France

Monaco

Workers making Renault cars in a huge factory near Paris.

The Eiffel Tower was built in 1889 for the Great Exhibition. It is made of iron and is 400 metres high. A spectacular view of Paris can be seen from the higher levels of the tower.

The beautiful Chateau de Chenonceaux is in the Loire Valley.

GREAT BRITAIN

NORTH SEA

Kilometres

0 50 100 150 200 Kilometres

0 50 100 150 Miles

Miles

ENGLISH CHANNEL

Dunkerque
Calais
Boulogne

Roubaix
Lille
Douai
Valenciennes

BELGIUM

LUXEM-
BOURG

GERMANY

Dieppe
Somme Amiens
Le Havre
Cherbourg
Rouen
Caen
Channel Islands
Seine

Oise
Meuse

Reims
Metz
Nancy
Strasbourg

Brest

Paris
Versailles
Chartres
Fontainebleau
Marne

Champagne

Vosges Mts

Rennes
Le Mans

Mulhouse

Angers
Orleans
Loire

Nantes
Tours

Saône

Dijon

Bourgogne
(Burgundy)

SWITZERLAND

F R A N C E

Jura Mts

Limoges

Lyon

Mt Blanc
4807m

Clermont-Ferrand
▲ Mt Dore
1886m
Saint-Etienne

Grenoble

French Alps

Périgueux

Massif Central

ITALY

BAY OF BISCAY

Bordeaux
Dordogne

Rhône

Cevennes Mts

▲2710 m

CORSICA
(France)

Garonne

Nîmes
Avignon
Montpellier
Arles

Nice
MONACO
Cannes

Corsica is an island
belonging to France. To
see its proper location
turn to page 29.

Bayonne
Biarritz
Lourdes

Toulouse

Marseille
Toulon

Carcassonne
Narbonne

P y r e n e e s

Perpignan

ANDORRA

SPAIN

MEDITERRANEAN SEA

21

Germany

Germany became a united country again in 1990, after having been divided into two countries – East and West Germany – for 45 years. At the end of World War II in 1945, Germany was divided into four zones. The USA, the UK and France occupied three zones in the west; the USSR occupied the eastern zone. The eastern zone became East Germany, closely linked with the USSR. The rest of the country and West Berlin formed West Germany, with its capital at Bonn. The USSR erected the Berlin Wall to divide the two countries.

Germany now has nearly 80 million people – far more than any other European country apart from the USSR. Most of the western part is rich, with many modern industries manufacturing everything from steel to textiles, cars, heavy machinery and electrical equipment. In the poorer eastern part, the factories are being modernized where possible. Farming is important.

Germany

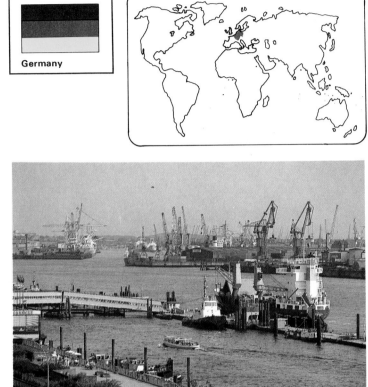

Above: Hamburg is a major docking point in the North Sea.

Left: Until 1989, the Brandenburg Gate was part of the dividing line between East and West Berlin.

Below: Barges travel down the Rhine past lovely towns and castles, green fields and vineyards.

Kilometres
0   50   100   150
0   30   60   90
Miles

N

BALTIC SEA

NORTH SEA

Kiel Canal

●Kiel

●Rostock

●Lubeck

●Hamburg

Elbe

Erns

●Bremen

POLAND

Oder

Aller

Weser

Hanover●   ■ **Berlin**

Brunswick●

Magdeburg●

Oder

NETHERLANDS

Munster●   ●Bieleteld

H a r z   M t s

Spree

Elbe

Neisse

Dortmund
Essen●●Bochum   Halle●
Duisburg●
Krefeld●   ●Wuppertal   Kassel●   Leipzig●
Monchen-gladbach   ●Dusseldorf
Ruhr

●Cologne   **G E R M A N Y**   Dresden●

●Aachen   ●Bonn   Karl-Marx-Stadt●

BELGIUM

CZECHOSLOVAKIA

●Frankfurt
Wiesbaden●
●Mainz

Mosel

LUXEMBOURG

Main

●Mannheim   ●Nuremberg

●Saarbrucken

Rhine

●Karlsruhe

B l a c k   F o r e s t

●Stuttgart   Danube

FRANCE

●Augsberg

●Munich

SWITZERLAND   AUSTRIA

23

Switzerland and Austria

Switzerland and Austria are well known for their snow-capped mountains called the Alps. The Alps attract many visitors who like to ski in the winter and visit lakes, glaciers and alpine meadows full of wild flowers in the summer. Long tunnels and bridges take roads and railways through the mountains and valleys.

In Switzerland rivers are dammed to catch water and make electricity for homes and factories. This is called *hydroelectricity*. Many Swiss people work in factories making chemicals, scientific instruments, clocks and watches and delicious chocolate. Banks and hotels provide important jobs.

Most Swiss people speak German, but French, Italian and Romansch are also spoken.

Austria was part of a large and important country called the Austro-Hungarian Empire until 1918. Now it is quite small. Austria has some minerals such as iron and oil, but tourism is also very important. Most Austrians live in towns. Vienna, the capital, is famous for its music. In the past famous musicians such as Beethoven and Mozart have lived and composed music there.

Sandwiched between Austria and Switzerland is the tiny country of Liechtenstein.

Holiday resorts in Switzerland are well known for their fresh mountain air and clear lakes. In the summer, boating and mountain climbing are popular activities.

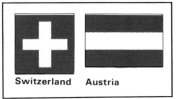

Switzerland   Austria

Left: Among the many large lakes in Switzerland is Lake Luzern.

Right: Ice skating out of doors is possible for many months in alpine countries.

Below: An outdoor cafe in a busy Vienna shopping district provides a meeting place for friends.

CZECHOSLOVAKIA

Kilometres
0   50   100   150   200

0   50   100
Miles

GERMANY

FRANCE

Basel

Jura Mts   Aare   Zurich

Berne   Luzern

SWITZERLAND   Rhine   LIECHTENSTEIN

4274 m

4094 m

Lake Leman
(L. Geneva)   Lausanne

Geneva   Rhone   The Alps

Matterhorn
4478 m

4634 m

Lake Constance

Inn   Innsbruck

ITALY

Linz   Danube

Vienna

Salzburg   AUSTRIA

Enns

Gross
Glockner
3797

Graz

HUNGARY

YUGOSLAVIA

Spain and Portugal

Spain's interior is a vast *plateau*, which means an area of high flat ground. It is crossed by several mountain ranges. But the highest peaks are in the Pyrenees in the north and the Sierra Nevada in the south. Fertile plains and sandy beaches surround the central plateau. Spain is divided into several regions. One of these is Andalusia in the south. It is famous for its lively fiestas and gypsy flamenco dancers.

Spain's warm climate and golden sands attract thousands of tourists to its coastal resorts. Many Spaniards work in the tourist industry, but most work on the land. Some farmers do everything by hand or with the help of a donkey or mule. The soil is very dry and needs to be constantly watered, or *irrigated*. Farmers grow wheat, rice, olives, grapes and oranges.

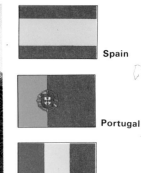

Spain

Portugal

Andorra

Top: Roman walls surround a city in Castile, a region in central Spain. The Romans ruled in Spain for six hundred years.

Middle: Workers in Portugal gather bark from cork trees to make cork.

Far left: Tourists relax on the warm, sunny beaches of Ibiza.

Left: A fisherman mends his net in Albufeira, Portugal. Huge numbers of sardines are caught off Portugal's coast.

Portugal borders Spain on the west. Most people are fishermen and farmers. Others work in the tourist industry or in factories where they process food and make textiles. There are large cork forests in Portugal and many vineyards. Cork and port, a special type of wine, are exported to countries all over the world.

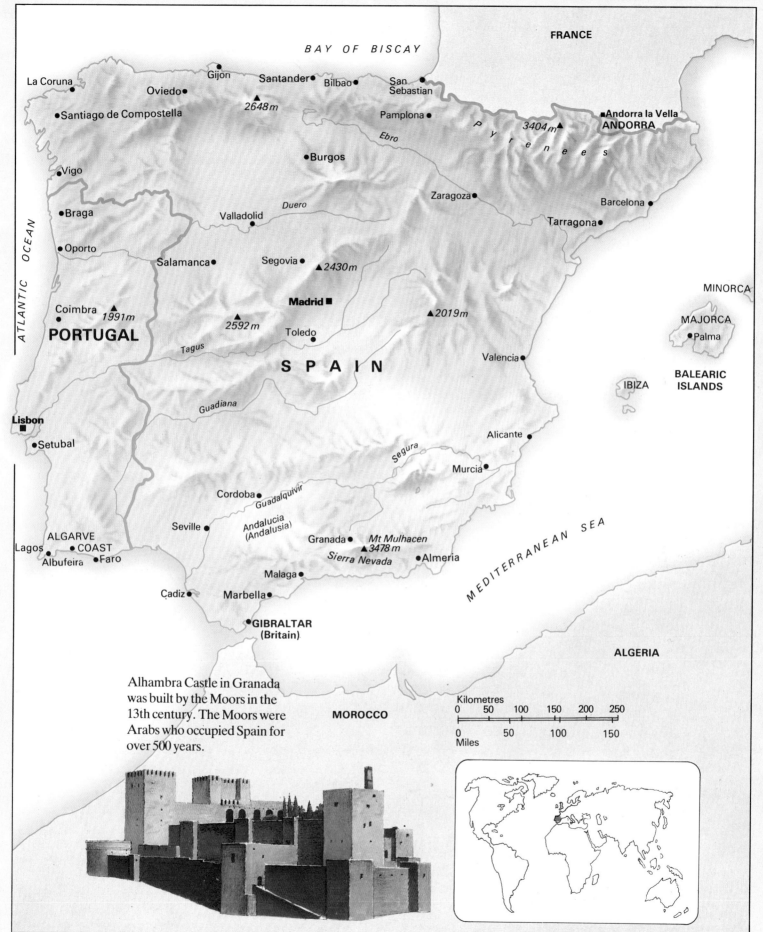

FRANCE

BAY OF BISCAY

La Coruna

Gijon

Santander

Bilbao

San Sebastian

Oviedo

▲ 2648m

Pamplona

Pyrenees

▲ 3404m

■ Andorra la Vella
ANDORRA

Santiago de Compostella

Ebro

Vigo

Burgos

Zaragoza

Barcelona

Duero

Braga

Valladolid

Tarragona

Oporto

Salamanca

Segovia

▲ 2430m

Coimbra

▲ 1991m

PORTUGAL

Madrid ■

▲ 2592 m

Toledo

▲ 2019m

ATLANTIC OCEAN

Tagus

S P A I N

MINORCA

MAJORCA

Palma

Valencia

BALEARIC ISLANDS

Guadiana

IBIZA

Lisbon ■

Setubal

Alicante

Segura

Murcia

Cordoba

Guadalquivir

ALGARVE COAST

Lagos

Albufeira

Faro

Seville

Andalucia (Andalusia)

Granada

Mt Mulhacen

▲ 3478 m

Sierra Nevada

Almeria

MEDITERRANEAN SEA

Malaga

Cadiz

Marbella

GIBRALTAR
(Britain)

ALGERIA

Alhambra Castle in Granada
was built by the Moors in the
13th century. The Moors were
Arabs who occupied Spain for
over 500 years.

MOROCCO

Kilometres

0   50   100   150   200   250

0   50   100   150

Miles

Italy and its Neighbours

Italy is shaped like a boot kicking a ball. Sicily is the 'ball'. Sicily, Sardinia and many smaller islands are also part of Italy. The Apennine Mountains run down the back of Italy like a spine. There are several volcanic mountains in Italy. The best known is Mount Vesuvius, near the city of Naples in southern Italy.

Tourists flock to Italy to enjoy the warm climate, to see the beautiful buildings and paintings, and to visit the ruins of Ancient Rome. In the north there are large industrial cities, such as Milan and Turin. Italians make textiles and cars for *export*, to sell to other countries. In the south farmers grow olives, citrus fruit, and grapes for making wine.

Vatican City is the smallest country in Europe. It is the home of the Pope, the head of the Roman Catholic Church. San Marino is another tiny country in Italy and Malta is an island country in the Mediterranean Sea.

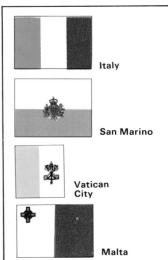

Italy

San Marino

Vatican City

Malta

Above: St. Peter's Square is in Vatican City.
Left: Venice has many fine churches like Santa Maria della Salute. Boats called *gondolas* take people from place to place on canals that run through the city.
Right: The Leaning Tower of Pisa.

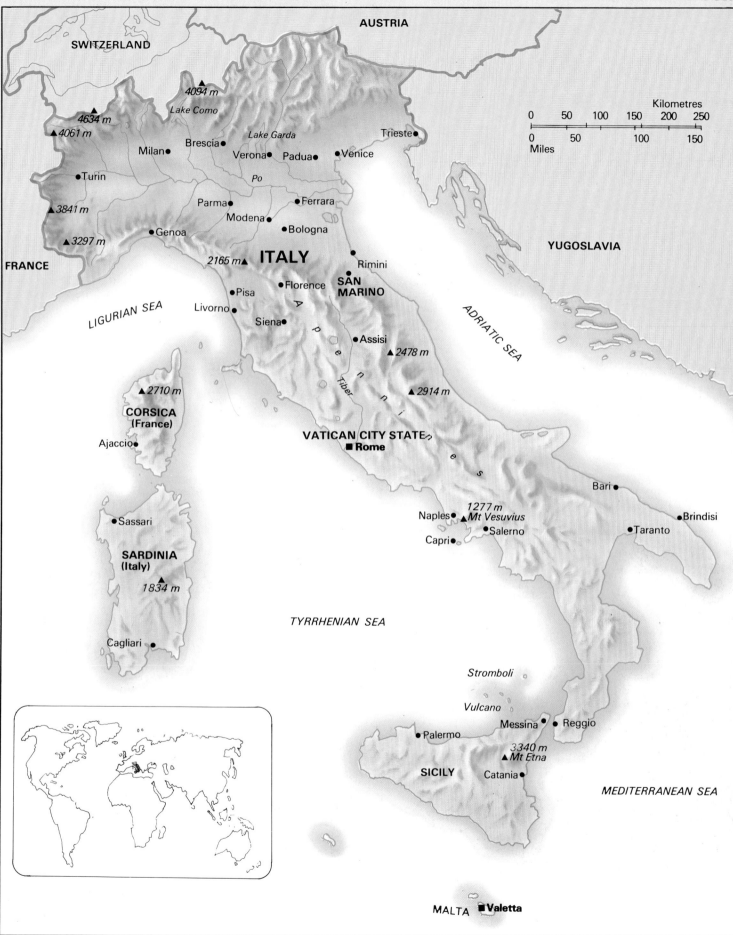

SWITZERLAND

AUSTRIA

▲ 4094 m

Lake Como

▲ 4634 m

▲ 4061 m

Milan ● Brescia ● Verona ● Padua ● ● Venice

● Turin *Po*

Lake Garda

Trieste ●

● Genoa

Parma ● Modena ● ● Ferrara

● Bologna

▲ 3841 m

▲ 3297 m

FRANCE

YUGOSLAVIA

2165 m ▲ **ITALY**

Rimini ●

● Pisa Florence ● **SAN MARINO**

Livorno ● Siena ●

LIGURIAN SEA

A p e n n i n e s

Assisi ●

▲ 2478 m

Tiber

ADRIATIC SEA

▲ 2710 m

▲ 2914 m

CORSICA (France)

Ajaccio ●

VATICAN CITY STATE

■ **Rome**

● Sassari

Bari ●

SARDINIA (Italy)

Naples ● 1277 m
▲ *Mt Vesuvius*

Brindisi ●

Capri ● ● Salerno

Taranto ●

▲ 1834 m

TYRRHENIAN SEA

● Cagliari

Stromboli

Vulcano

Messina ● ● Reggio

Palermo ●

3340 m
▲ *Mt Etna*

SICILY Catania ●

MEDITERRANEAN SEA

MALTA ■ **Valetta**

Poland, Czechoslovakia and Hungary

Poland and Hungary are countries with vast areas of flat land. The fertile lowlands are good for farming and herds of cattle and horses graze on the wide open plains. Between these two countries lies Czechoslovakia. Here the snow-capped Carpathian Mountains tower over the land.

Poland is the largest country. It is a major world producer of coal. There are many big ports on the Baltic Sea where ships are built. Czechoslovakia and Hungary do not have any seaside but the River Danube links them with the sea. Potatoes, wheat and sugar-beet are important crops. Since 1945 more Poles, Czechs and Hungarians have been leaving the farms to work in industry. Czechoslovakia, Poland and Hungary were communist countries from 1945, but, in 1989, the people demanded and achieved a more democratic form of government.

Poland

Czechoslovakia

Hungary

A view of Prague, capital of Czechoslovakia, in winter.

Above: Czechoslovakia is a country of mountains, basins and valleys.
Right: Buda and Pest are shown with the River Danube in between. Together they make Budapest, the capital of Hungary.

Workers harvest their crops on a collective farm in Poland.

LITHUANIA

BALTIC SEA

Gdansk

Szczecin

Bydgoszcz

Netze

Oder

Poznan

Warta

Vistula

Bug

Warsaw

POLAND

Lodz

Neisse

Wroclaw

Lublin

Katowice

Krakow

Prague *Elbe*

Plzen

1492

Ostrava

Carpathian Mts

CZECHOSLOVAKIA

Vltava

Brno

Van

2655

Kosice

GERMANY

USSR

Bratislava

Miskolc

AUSTRIA

Danube

Budapest

Debrecen

Tisza

Lake Balaton

HUNGARY

ROMANIA

ITALY

Pecs

Szeged

YUGOSLAVIA

0   50   100   150   200 Kilometres

0   50   100
Miles

The Balkans and Romania

Bulgaria, Yugoslavia, Albania and Greece make up the Balkan countries. Romania borders Bulgaria and Yugoslavia.

Greece consists of the mainland and over 1400 islands. It is very mountainous and sheep and goats graze over the hills. Only one-third of Greece is suitable for farming. But in spite of this nearly half of the people live on the land. Many farmers grow grapes for making wine. Sometimes the grapes are picked, left to dry in the hot sun, then sold as raisins, currants or sultanas.

Bulgaria, Yugoslavia, Albania and Romania are also very mountainous. But, unlike Greece, the mountains are covered with forests where wolves, wild boars and bears still live. Beneath the valuable forests there are rich deposits of copper, zinc, coal and oil. Many people work in industry turning these minerals into useful products. Many others, especially in Albania, work on farms in the valleys.

Yugoslavia and Greece have beautiful beaches and islands. Thousands of holiday-makers go there each year. Greece also has fascinating ruins from the times of the Ancient Greeks.

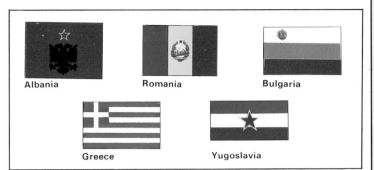

Albania   Romania   Bulgaria

Greece   Yugoslavia

Above: The Parthenon in Athens was built by the Ancient Greeks.
Left: Many Romanians work on farms growing maize, wheat and tobacco. They also raise sheep.
Below: Dubrovnik, in Yugoslavia, is well known for its beaches and medieval buildings.

Kilometres

| 0 | 50 | 100 | 150 | 200 | 250 |

Miles

| 0 | 50 | 100 | 150 |

USSR

HUNGARY

▲ Mt Triglav
2863m
Ljubljana •

Drava

• Zagreb

Tisa

• Timisoara

Cluj •

Carpathian Mts

Iasi •

• Brasov

2543m ▲

Transylvania Alps

Galati •

• Rijeka

Sava

Dinaric Alps

YUGOSLAVIA

• Sarajevo

Morava

Turnu
Severin
• Belgrade

2518m ▲

ROMANIA

• Ploesti

• Craiova

Bucharest ■

Constanta •

Danube
• Ruse

BLACK
SEA

• Split

▲2522m

• Nis

Iskar

Sofia ■

BULGARIA

• Varna

ADRIATIC
SEA

• Dubrovnik

Balkan Mts

▲
2692m

2496m
▲

• Skopje

Vardar

Mt
Musala
2925m ▲

Marits a
• Plovdiv

Rhodope Mts

• Burgas

Tirana ■

2480m
▲

ALBANIA

Thessaloniki •

2637m
▲

Mt Olympus
▲ 2917m

Pindus Mts

• Trikkala

GREECE

• Delphi

• Patras

AEGEAN
SEA

LESVOS

TURKEY

2376m ▲

Athens ■
Piraeus ■

MYKONOS

• Corinth

• Olympia

IONIAN SEA

Kalamata •

• Sparta

NAXOS

This picture shows a
windmill on the Greek
island of Mykonos.
Whitewashed buildings
like those in the
background are often
found in Greece.

MEDITERRANEAN SEA

RHODES

CRETE • Iraklion

33

USSR and the Baltics

The Union of Soviet Socialist Republics, the USSR, is the largest country in the world. It is more than twice the size of Canada, the second largest country, and covers one-sixth of the world's total land surface. The Baltic States include Estonia, Latvia and Lithuania.

One-quarter of the USSR is farmland. Farmers work either on enormous state-owned farms or on smaller *collectives*. The USSR is a leading producer of wheat, meat and dairy products. It also has large *resources* of coal, oil and natural gas. These provide fuel for the huge numbers of factories and industrial plants.

The USSR is made up of people of over 100 groups – Ukranians, Uzbeks, Kazakhs and many others. Over 60 languages are spoken. Until 1991, the USSR was divided into 15 republics, Russia being the largest. In 1991, Communist rule ended and the Baltic States, formerly Soviet republics, gained their independence. Other republics also want to be recognized as independent states.

Map labels: NORWEGIAN SEA, SWEDEN, FINLAND, Murmansk, Arkhangelsk, Tallinn, ESTONIA, St. Petersburg, Riga, LATVIA, U, LITHUANIA, Vilnius, Steppes, POLAND, Minsk, Moscow, Gorki, Kiev, Kuybyshe, Ural, Dnieper, Kharkov, Don, Volga, Kishinev, Donetsk, Volgograd, ROMANIA, Odessa, Astrakhan, Sevastopol, CASPIAN SEA, BLACK SEA, Caucasus, ARA SEA, Mt Elbrus, 5633m, is the highest mountain in Europe, Tbilisi, Yerevan, Baku, Kara Kum, Askhabad, IRAN

Flags: Estonia, Lithuania, Latvia, USSR

Left: Melons are sold at the market in Samarkand, in the south of the USSR.

Right: On huge state farms in the Steppes wheat is harvested by combines. Most people live on farms and in cities west of the Ural mountains. Farther east over the mountains there are high plains and vast forests. The Trans-Siberian Railway runs from Moscow in the west to Vladivostok in the east – over 9000 kilometres.

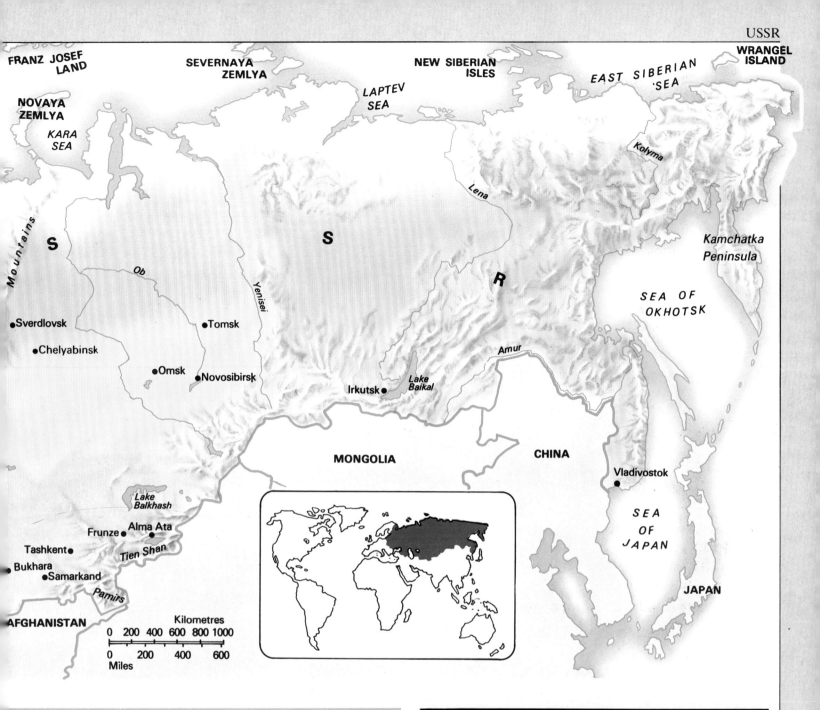

FRANZ JOSEF LAND

SEVERNAYA ZEMLYA

NEW SIBERIAN ISLES

WRANGEL ISLAND

NOVAYA ZEMLYA

KARA SEA

LAPTEV SEA

EAST SIBERIAN SEA

Kolyma

Mountains

S

S

Lena

Kamchatka Peninsula

•Sverdlovsk

Ob

Yenisei

R

SEA OF OKHOTSK

•Chelyabinsk

•Tomsk

•Omsk

•Novosibirsk

Amur

Irkutsk• Lake Baikal

MONGOLIA

CHINA

Vladivostok•

SEA OF JAPAN

Lake Balkhash

Frunze• Alma Ata

Tien Shan

Tashkent•

Bukhara•

•Samarkand

Pamirs

AFGHANISTAN

JAPAN

Kilometres
0 200 400 600 800 1000

0 200 400 600
Miles

Above: Inside the Kremlin (Russian for fortress) is the national museum. Lenin's tomb is in the foreground.
Left: Red Square and St Basil's Cathedral in Moscow.

South-West Asia

Most people living in the Middle East are Arab. Their language is Arabic and their religion is Islam. Even in the non-Arab countries, Iran and Turkey, the people are Muslim. Many Christians live in Cyprus and Lebanon and most of the people in Israel are Jewish. The different religions of the people living in this area is the cause of constant trouble between them.

On the map you can see that most of this area is desert. Many of the people are farmers and the lack of rainfall is a serious problem.

On the Mediterranean coast, in river valleys and around *oases*, farms are irrigated with water from rivers and wells. But it is oil and not farming which has brought wealth to many countries in this area.

Every year pilgrims arrive in the Middle East. Jerusalem, the capital of Israel, is regarded as a holy city by Jews, Christians and Muslims. Mecca and Medina in Saudi Arabia are Muslim holy cities.

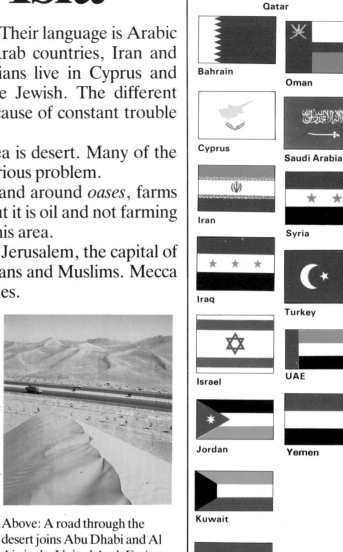

Qatar

Bahrain

Oman

Cyprus

Saudi Arabia

Iran

Syria

Iraq

Turkey

Israel

UAE

Jordan

Yemen

Kuwait

Lebanon

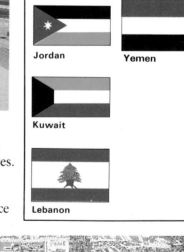

Above: A road through the desert joins Abu Dhabi and Al Ain in the United Arab Emirates.

Below: Muslims make their pilgrimage to Mecca, birthplace of the prophet Muhammad.

Jews pray at the Wailing Wall in the Old City of Jerusalem. The Dome of the Rock, sacred to Muslims, is in the background.

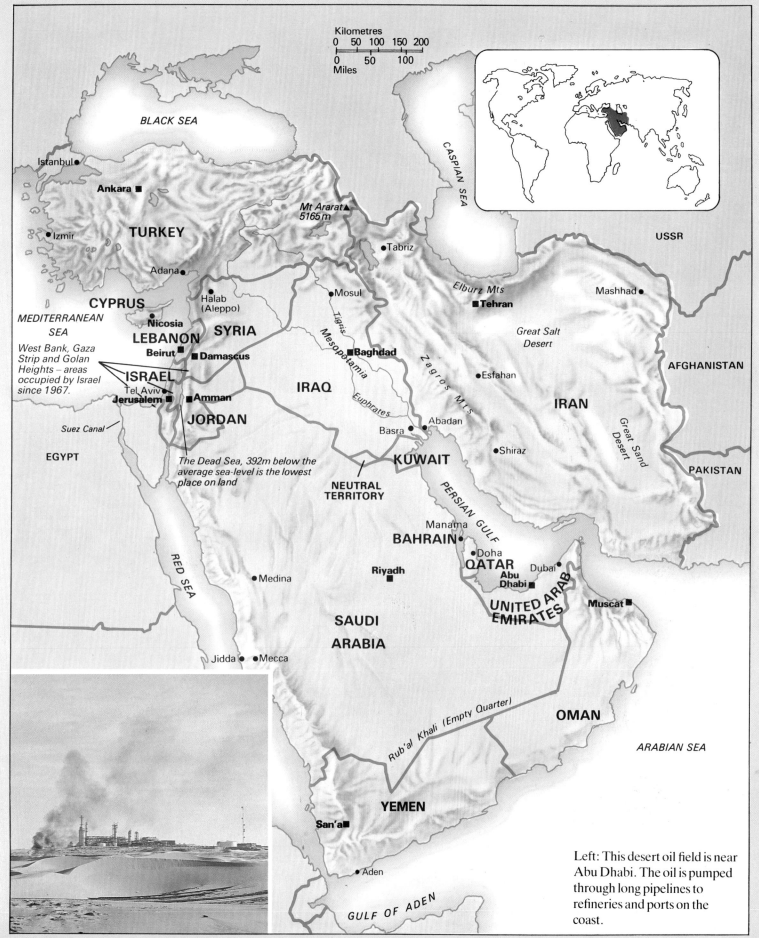

Kilometres
0 50 100 150 200
0   50   100
Miles

BLACK SEA

Istanbul •

Ankara ■

Izmir •

TURKEY

Adana •

Mt Ararat ▲
5165 m

CASPIAN SEA

USSR

• Tabriz

CYPRUS

Halab
(Aleppo) •

• Mosul

Elburz Mts

Mashhad •

■ **Tehran**

MEDITERRANEAN
SEA

Nicosia •

SYRIA

Tigris

Great Salt
Desert

West Bank, Gaza
Strip and Golan
Heights – areas
occupied by Israel
since 1967.

LEBANON

Beirut •

■ **Damascus**

Mesopotamia

■ **Baghdad**

Zagros Mts

AFGHANISTAN

ISRAEL

Tel Aviv •

IRAQ

Euphrates

Esfahan •

IRAN

Great Sand
Desert

Jerusalem ■

■ **Amman**

JORDAN

Basra •

• Abadan

Suez Canal

The Dead Sea, 392m below the
average sea-level is the lowest
place on land

Shiraz •

PAKISTAN

EGYPT

NEUTRAL
TERRITORY

KUWAIT

RED SEA

PERSIAN GULF

• Medina

Riyadh •

Manama •

BAHRAIN ■

Doha •

QATAR

Dubai •

**Abu
Dhabi** ■

Muscat ■

UNITED ARAB
EMIRATES

SAUDI

ARABIA

Jidda • • Mecca

Rub 'al Khali (Empty Quarter)

OMAN

ARABIAN SEA

YEMEN

San'a ■

Left: This desert oil field is near
Abu Dhabi. The oil is pumped
through long pipelines to
refineries and ports on the
coast.

• Aden

GULF OF ADEN

37

India and its Neighbours

This region contains the highest mountain range in the world – the Himalayas. It forms the boundary with Tibet and China and contains Mount Everest, the world's highest peak. On the map opposite you can trace the paths of three great rivers. They begin in the Himalayas and are the Ganges, the Indus and the Brahmaputra.

India, Pakistan and Bangladesh are thickly populated nations. Farming is the main occupation, but there is never enough food for the huge numbers of people. Many children start to work in the fields with their parents when they are very young. Farming methods are often very simple because there is little money for machinery or fertilizers. The *monsoon* climate is also a problem. It means that twice a year there are huge downpours of rain. If the rain is too heavy, it washes away crops. If the rains come too late, the crops may die. The Indian, Pakistani and Bangladeshi governments are trying to set up more factories.

Religion is important in the everyday life of the people in this region. Most Indians are Hindu while most Pakistanis and Afghanis and many Bangladeshis are Muslim, followers of Islam.

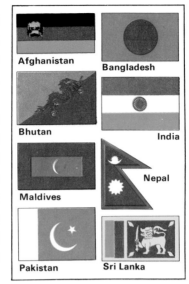

Afghanistan   Bangladesh
Bhutan   India
Nepal
Maldives
Pakistan   Sri Lanka

Above: Pilgrims bathe in the river Ganges at Varanasi, the Hindus' holy city.

Above right: The Taj Mahal is made of white marble. It is the tomb of a Mogul Emperor and his favourite wife.

Right: This film poster is in New Delhi. More films are made in India than in any other country.

Far right: Women pick tea leaves in Darjeeling. Behind them is Mount Kanchenjunga.

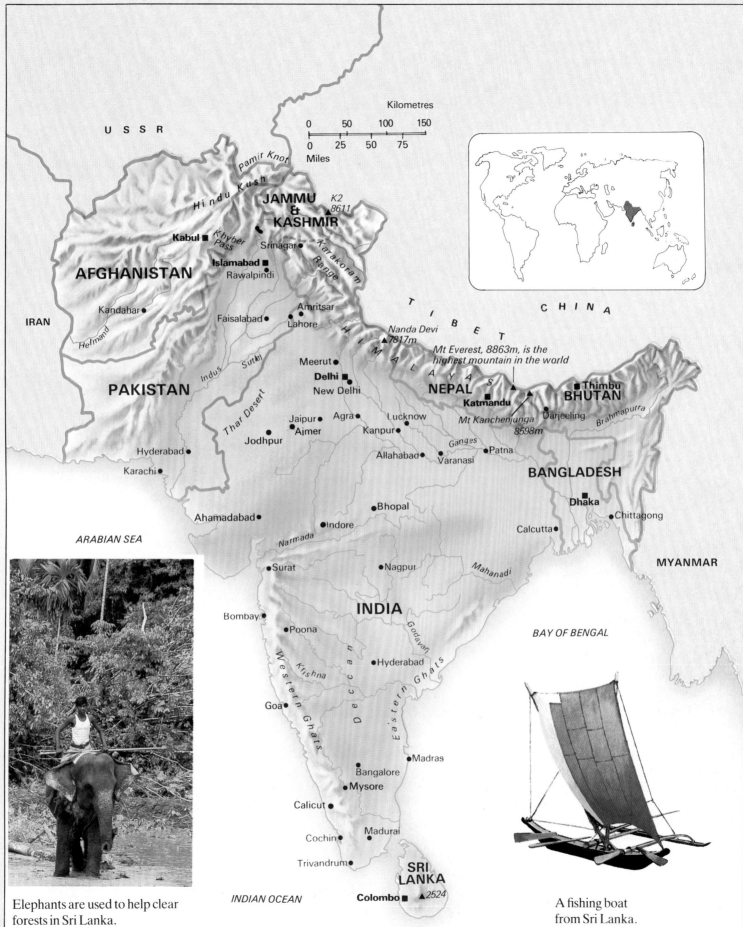

Kilometres

| 0 | 50 | 100 | 150 |

Miles

| 0 | 25 | 50 | 75 |

U S S R

Pamir Knot

Hindu Kush

JAMMU & KASHMIR

K2 ▲ 8611

Kabul ■

Khyber Pass

Srinagar ●

AFGHANISTAN

Islamabad ■

Rawalpindi

Karakoram Range

T I B E T

C H I N A

IRAN

Kandahar ●

Helmand

Faisalabad ●

Amritsar ●

Lahore ●

H I M A L A Y A S

Nanda Devi ▲ 7817m

Mt Everest, 8863m, is the highest mountain in the world

PAKISTAN

Indus

Sutlej

Meerut ●

Delhi ■

New Delhi

NEPAL

Katmandu ■

Mt Kanchenjunga 8598m

Thimbu ■

BHUTAN

Darjeeling

Brahmaputra

Thar Desert

Jaipur ●

Agra ●

Ajmer ●

Jodhpur ●

Lucknow ●

Kanpur ●

Allahabad ●

Ganges

Varanasi ●

Patna ●

BANGLADESH

Hyderabad ●

Dhaka ■

Chittagong ●

Karachi ●

Ahamadabad ●

Bhopal ●

Indore ●

Calcutta ●

ARABIAN SEA

Narmada

Surat ●

Nagpur ●

Mahanadi

MYANMAR

Bombay ●

INDIA

Poona ●

BAY OF BENGAL

Godavari

Hyderabad ●

Deccan

Krishna

Goa ●

Western Ghats

Eastern Ghats

Madras ●

Bangalore ●

Mysore ●

Calicut ●

Cochin ●

Madurai ●

Trivandrum ●

SRI LANKA

Colombo ■ ▲ 2524

INDIAN OCEAN

Elephants are used to help clear forests in Sri Lanka.

A fishing boat from Sri Lanka.

China

Nearly a quarter of all the people in the world live in China. It has more people than any other nation. Most people live in the fertile valleys of the Hwang Ho and Yangtze rivers and along the crowded coast. China is the third largest country in the world. It stretches from the plateau of Central Asia to the Pacific Ocean.

Since 1949, China has had a communist government. Mao Zedong (Mao Tse-tung) was the leader of the government until his death in 1976. By encouraging everyone to put the needs of the community first, he helped turn China from a poor agricultural country into a great industrial one. Factories have been built all over China and many of the workers make iron and steel. But farming is still important and two-thirds of the people are farmers.

Mongolia lies to the north of China. Most of the country is desert and the few people living there are wandering herdsmen. Many of them live in tents. On the map you can also see the peninsula of Korea. It is divided into two countries – North Korea and South Korea.

China

Mongolia

North Korea

South Korea

Above: The Great Wall of China is 2400 kilometres long. It was built 2500 years ago to keep Mongol invaders out.

Above right: A junk in Causeway Bay. Hong Kong has been a British Colony for many years but in 1997 it will return to China.

Right: Herdsmen in Mongolia lay the foundations for a tent or *yurt*.

Tien

Tarim

Kunlun

Himalaya

NEPA

INDIA

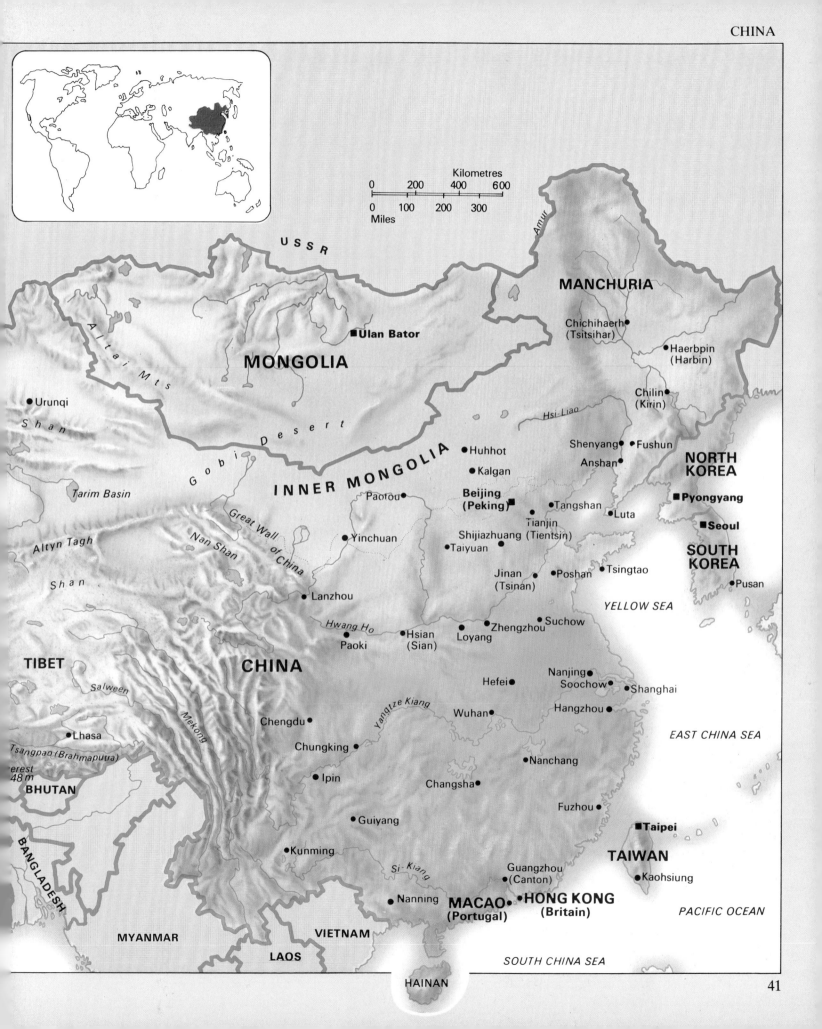

Kilometres
0   200   400   600

0   100   200   300
Miles

U S S R

MANCHURIA

MONGOLIA

■ Ulan Bator

Altai Mts

Shan

• Urunqi

Gobi Desert

Tarim Basin

INNER MONGOLIA

Chichihaerh
(Tsitsihar)

• Haerbpin
(Harbin)

Chilin
(Kirin)

Hsi-Liao

Amur

• Huhhot

• Kalgan

Shenyang • • Fushun
Anshan •

NORTH
KOREA

■ Pyongyang

Great Wall

Paotou

Beijing
(Peking) ■

Tangshan •
• Luta

Altyn Tagh

Nan Shan

• Yinchuan

of China

Shijiazhuang
• Taiyuan

Tianjin
(Tientsin)

■ Seoul

SOUTH
KOREA

Shan

• Lanzhou

Jinan
(Tsinan)

• Poshan

• Tsingtao

• Pusan

Hwang Ho

Paoki •

Hsian
(Sian)

• Loyang

• Zhengzhou

• Suchow

YELLOW SEA

TIBET

Salween

CHINA

Nanjing •
Hefei •   Soochow •

• Shanghai

• Lhasa

Mekong

Yangtze Kiang

Wuhan •

Hangzhou •

Tsangpao (Brahmaputra)

Chengdu •

EAST CHINA SEA

erest
48 m

BHUTAN

Chungking •

• Nanchang

• Ipin

Changsha •

BANGLADESH

• Guiyang

Fuzhou •

■ Taipei

• Kunming

TAIWAN

Si- Kiang

Guangzhou
• (Canton)

• Kaohsiung

• Nanning

MACAO
(Portugal)

• HONG KONG
(Britain)

PACIFIC OCEAN

MYANMAR

VIETNAM

LAOS

SOUTH CHINA SEA

HAINAN

41

Japan

Japan consists of four main islands and about 3000 smaller ones. From one end of the main islands to the other, there runs a volcanic mountain chain. Many of the volcanoes are still active. Mount Fuji, the highest peak, is a volcano, but it has not erupted since 1707. Earthquakes are common in Japan. There are over 1000 each year, but most of them are only small tremors.

There is not much land suitable for farming in Japan, because it is so mountainous. Rice is the main food crop on the little land which is cultivated. Fishing is important for it provides food for the large population. Japanese cooks use shark fins and eels to make soup and seaweed is also a favourite dish.

Japan is the wealthiest country in Asia because it has an efficient manufacturing industry. Japanese workers make more cameras, televisions and ships than any other country. There are many crowded industrial cities in Japan. But there are also peaceful temples and beautiful gardens.

Top: Television sets are checked on a conveyor belt in a Japanese factory. Other factories make cars, computers, watches, calculators and hi-fis.

Above: Workers harvest rice in Japan. Rice grows well on flat land where there is heavy rainfall.

Left: The bullet train is also called the 'Hikari Express'. It is the world's fastest passenger train and it travels between Tokyo and Osaka. Mount Fuji is in the background.

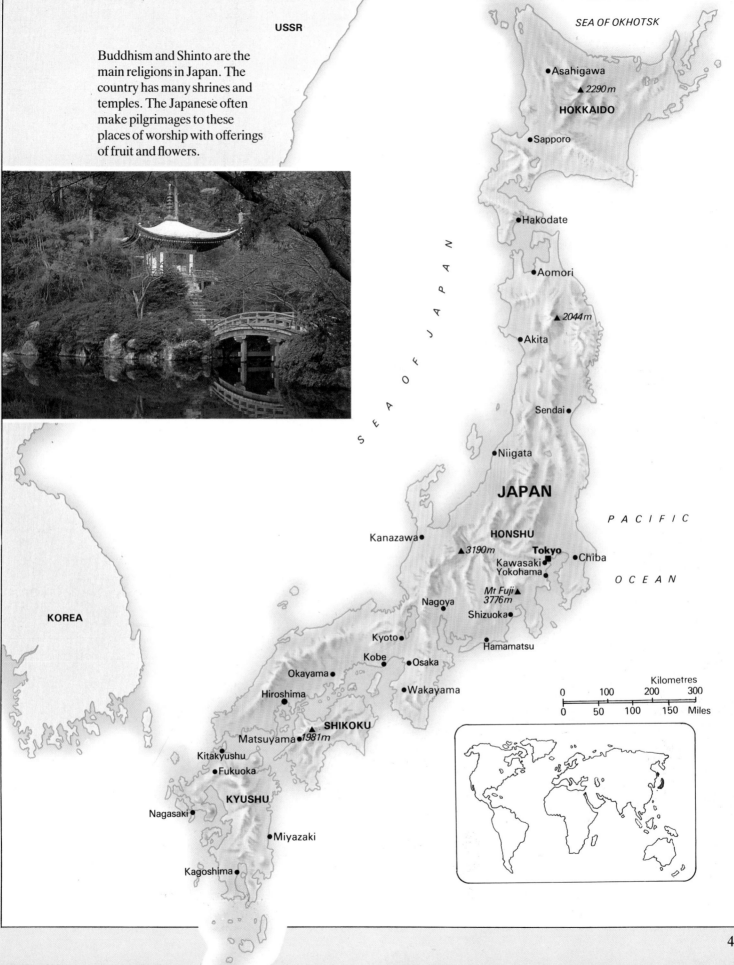

USSR

Buddhism and Shinto are the main religions in Japan. The country has many shrines and temples. The Japanese often make pilgrimages to these places of worship with offerings of fruit and flowers.

SEA OF OKHOTSK

•Asahigawa
▲2290m
HOKKAIDO

•Sapporo

•Hakodate

S E A   O F   J A P A N

•Aomori

▲2044m

•Akita

•Sendai

•Niigata

JAPAN

HONSHU

Kanazawa•

▲3190m

Tokyo
•Chiba
Kawasaki•
Yokohama•

Mt Fuji▲
3776m

Nagoya•

Shizuoka•

Kyoto•

Hamamatsu•

Kobe•   •Osaka

Okayama•

•Wakayama

Hiroshima•

▲ **SHIKOKU**

Matsuyama• *1981m*

Kitakyushu•

•Fukuoka

KYUSHU

Nagasaki•

•Miyazaki

Kagoshima•

KOREA

P A C I F I C

O C E A N

Kilometres
0   100   200   300
0   50   100   150 Miles

South-East Asia

Much of South-East Asia is made up of volcanic islands. Indonesia has over 13,000 islands and the Philippines more than 7000. All the countries have a similar hot, wet climate and much of the land is mountainous.

South-East Asia is a heavily populated region. Many people live in stilt houses in fertile river valleys. Peasant farmers cut terraces into the hillsides where they grow rice, the main food crop. The slopes which are not tilled are covered in forest. There are also large rubber, coffee and tobacco plantations in Indonesia, Malaysia and Myanmar

Mining is another important occupation in this region. Malaysia produces one-third of the world's supply of tin. It is one of the richest countries in South-East Asia. But many people in Vietnam and its neighbouring countries are very poor because of years of war.

Music, dance, drama and hand-made crafts keep alive the ancient stories and legends of South-East Asia. Islam and Buddhism are the main religions in this area.

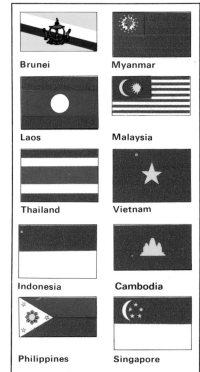

Brunei Myanmar
Laos Malaysia
Thailand Vietnam
Indonesia Cambodia
Philippines Singapore

Left: Fruit and vegetables are paddled in from the countryside and sold at the floating market in Bangkok. The many canals in the city are called *klongs*.

Right: Rice grows in paddies on terraced hillsides in the Philippines. It has been grown this way for hundreds of years.

Below: Huge figures of demons guard a Buddhist temple in Bangkok.

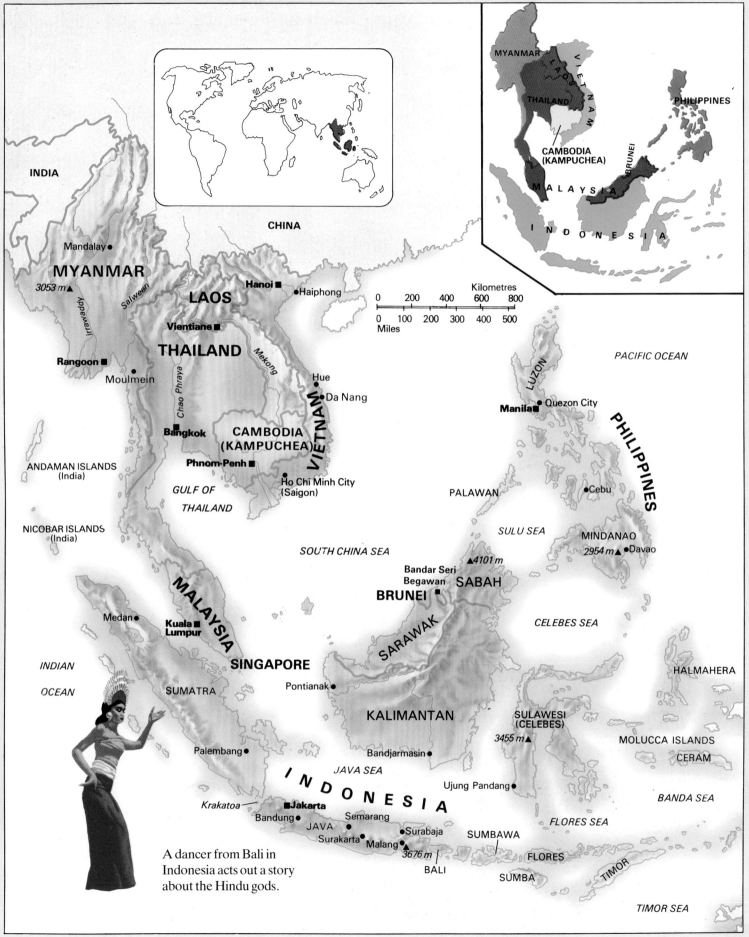

INDIA

MYANMAR
3053 m ▲
Mandalay ●

CHINA

LAOS

Hanoi ■
Haiphong ●

Salween
Irrawaddy
Appawadi

Vientiane ■

THAILAND

Rangoon ■
Moulmein ●

Chao Phraya
Mekong

Bangkok ■

VIETNAM

Hue ●
Da Nang ●

CAMBODIA
(KAMPUCHEA)

Phnom-Penh ■

Ho Chi Minh City
(Saigon) ●

GULF OF
THAILAND

ANDAMAN ISLANDS
(India)

NICOBAR ISLANDS
(India)

SOUTH CHINA SEA

Kilometres
0   200   400   600   800
0 100 200 300 400 500
Miles

PACIFIC OCEAN

LUZON

Manila ■ ● Quezon City

PHILIPPINES

● Cebu

PALAWAN

SULU SEA

MINDANAO
2954 m ▲ ● Davao

▲*4101 m*

Bandar Seri
Begawan ■
BRUNEI

SABAH

CELEBES SEA

MALAYSIA

Medan ●

Kuala
Lumpur ■

SINGAPORE

SUMATRA

SARAWAK

Pontianak ●

KALIMANTAN

HALMAHERA

INDIAN

OCEAN

SULAWESI
(CELEBES)

3455 m ▲

MOLUCCA ISLANDS

CERAM

Palembang ●

Bandjarmasin ●

JAVA SEA

INDONESIA

Ujung Pandang ●

BANDA SEA

Krakatoa

Jakarta ■
Bandung ●

Semarang ●

Surabaja ●

SUMBAWA

FLORES SEA

JAVA
Surakarta ●
Malang ▲
3676 m ▲
BALI

FLORES

SUMBA

TIMOR

TIMOR SEA

A dancer from Bali in
Indonesia acts out a story
about the Hindu gods.

MYANMAR
VIETNAM
LAOS
THAILAND
CAMBODIA
(KAMPUCHEA)
MALAYSIA
BRUNEI
PHILIPPINES
INDONESIA

45

Canada

Canada is the second largest country in the world. Only the USSR is larger. Vast areas in the far north are uninhabited and only a small number of trappers and fishermen live in the snow-blanketed forests around the Hudson Bay.

Most Canadians live in the south, not far from the USA border, where the climate is warmer. The Prairie Provinces of Manitoba, Saskatchewan and Alberta lie west of the Great Lakes. Sometimes they are called the 'food basket of the world' because wheat farms stretch as far as the eye can see.

Canada's original people arrived there over 20,000 years ago. They came from Asia and their descendants today are the North American Indians and the Inuit (Eskimos). British and French settlers did not arrive until the 17th century.

Large deposits of minerals as well as fertile plains and rich forests help make Canada one of the wealthiest countries in the world. Canadians are proud too, of their beautiful lakes and mountains and the cool, clean air of their forests.

Left: Lake Moraine is high in the Rockies in Banff National Park, Alberta.

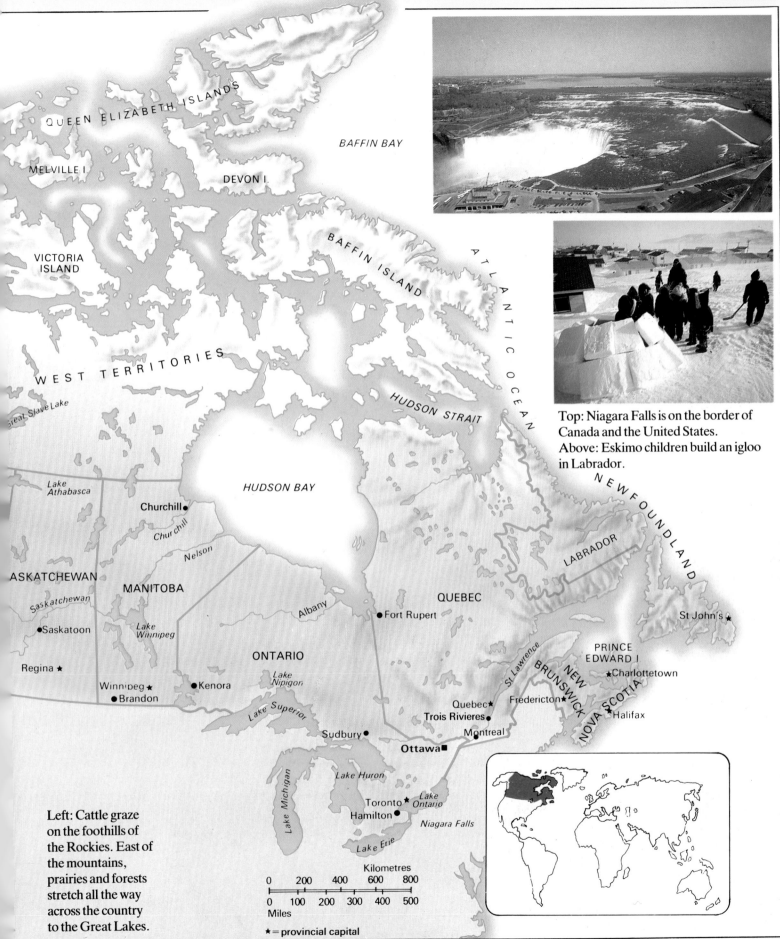

QUEEN ELIZABETH ISLANDS

BAFFIN BAY

MELVILLE I.

DEVON I.

VICTORIA ISLAND

BAFFIN ISLAND

W E S T   T E R R I T O R I E S

Great Slave Lake

A T L A N T I C   O C E A N

HUDSON STRAIT

HUDSON BAY

Lake Athabasca

Churchill •

Churchill

Nelson

NEWFOUNDLAND

LABRADOR

ASKATCHEWAN

MANITOBA

Saskatchewan

QUEBEC

• Saskatoon

Lake Winnipeg

Albany

• Fort Rupert

St John's ★

Regina ★

ONTARIO

PRINCE EDWARD I

★ Charlottetown

Winnipeg ★
• Brandon

Kenora •

Lake Nipigon

St Lawrence

NEW BRUNSWICK

Quebec ★
Fredericton •

Lake Superior

Trois Rivieres •

NOVA SCOTIA

• Halifax

Sudbury •

Montreal •

Ottawa ■

Lake Huron

Lake Michigan

Toronto ★

Lake Ontario

Hamilton •

Niagara Falls

Lake Erie

Top: Niagara Falls is on the border of Canada and the United States.
Above: Eskimo children build an igloo in Labrador.

Left: Cattle graze on the foothills of the Rockies. East of the mountains, prairies and forests stretch all the way across the country to the Great Lakes.

Kilometres

| 0 | 200 | 400 | 600 | 800 |

| 0 | 100 | 200 | 300 | 400 | 500 |

Miles

★ = provincial capital

USA

The United States of America is the fourth largest country in the world and has the fourth largest population and land area. It is divided into 50 states and includes Alaska in the north-west and Hawaii, a group of islands in the Pacific Ocean.

Like Canada, the USA was first settled by Indians whose ancestors came from Asia. In the 18th and 19th centuries, large numbers of settlers came to the 'New World' from Europe in search of a better way of life. These people first settled on the east coast and started the first thirteen states. Negroes were brought over from Africa to work on cotton and tobacco plantations in the south.

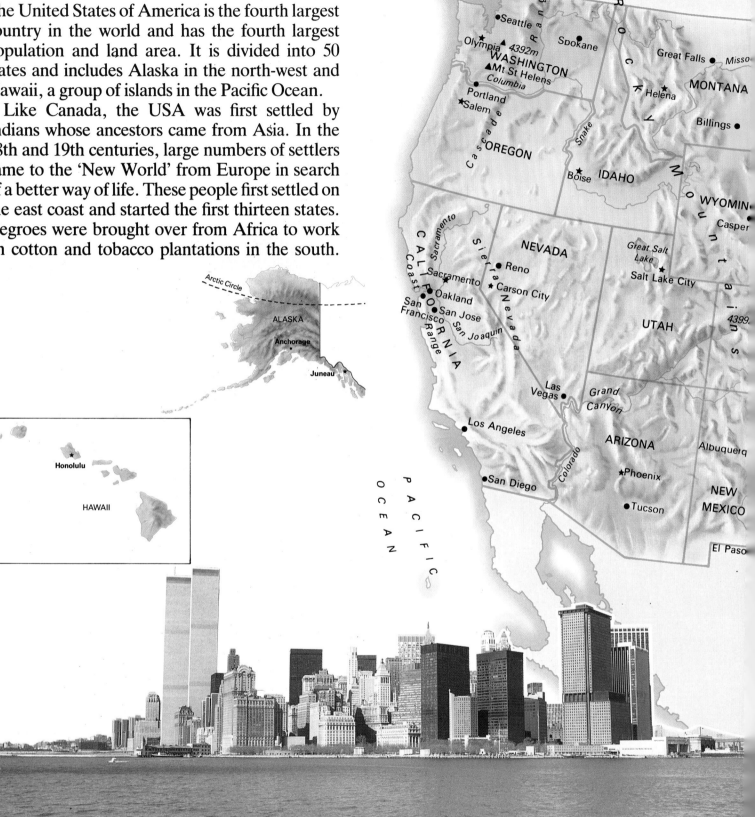

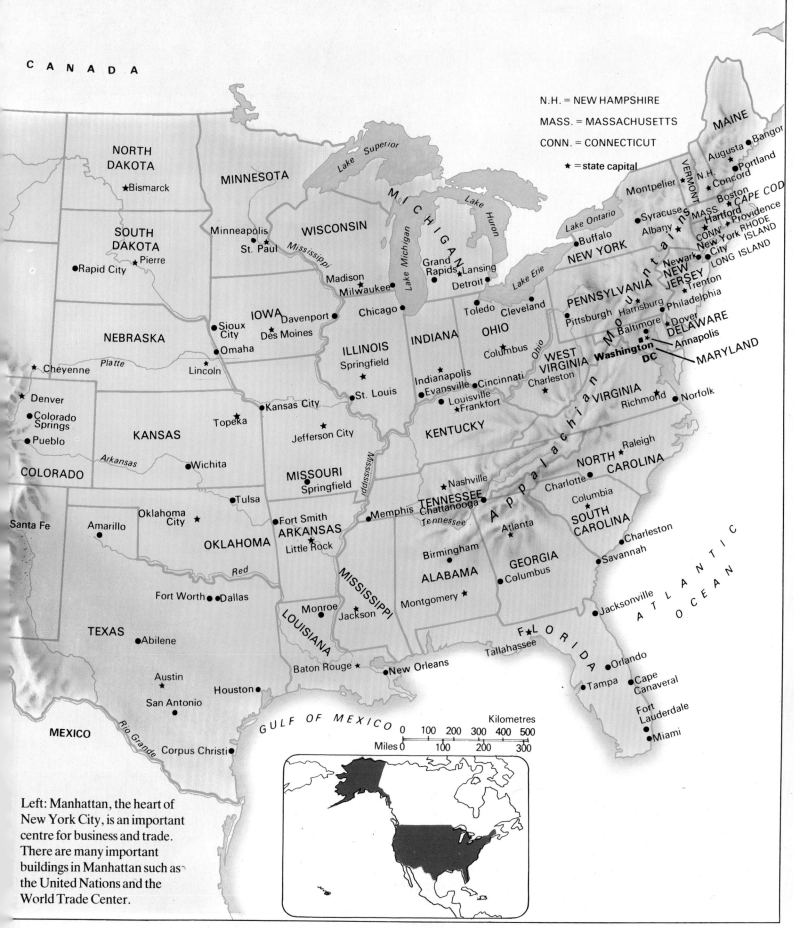

USA

CANADA

NORTH DAKOTA
★Bismarck

MINNESOTA

Lake Superior

MAINE

N.H. = NEW HAMPSHIRE
MASS. = MASSACHUSETTS
CONN. = CONNECTICUT

★ = state capital

Augusta ●Bangor

●Portland
Concord

VERMONT
Montpelier ★ ★ N.H.
★Boston
Albany Syracuse● MASS. Hartford CAPE COD
●Buffalo ★ CONN.★ ★Providence
New York RHODE
NEW YORK City ISLAND
LONG ISLAND

SOUTH DAKOTA
●Rapid City
★Pierre

●Minneapolis
St. Paul★
●

WISCONSIN
Mississippi

Lake Huron

MICHIGAN

Lake Michigan

Grand ●Rapids ●Lansing

Madison●
Milwaukee●

●Detroit

Lake Erie

Newark●
★●Trenton
NEW
JERSEY
●Philadelphia

NEBRASKA

●Sioux City
Des Moines●

IOWA
●Davenport

Chicago●

Toledo● Cleveland●

PENNSYLVANIA
●Pittsburgh Harrisburg★
●Baltimore★ Dover
DELAWARE
●Annapolis

●Omaha

ILLINOIS
Springfield
★

INDIANA

OHIO
●Columbus

Ohio

WEST VIRGINIA
●Charleston

Washington
DC

MARYLAND

★Cheyenne
●Lincoln

Platte

Kansas City●

Indianapolis★
Evansville● ●Cincinnati
●Louisville
★Frankfort

★Richmond
VIRGINIA ●Norfolk

★Denver
●Colorado Springs
●Pueblo

COLORADO

Arkansas

●Topeka

KANSAS

Jefferson City★

St. Louis★

●Wichita

MISSOURI
Springfield
●

KENTUCKY

★Nashville
●Charlotte

●Raleigh

NORTH CAROLINA

Santa Fe

●Amarillo

Oklahoma City★

Tulsa●

Fort Smith●

ARKANSAS
★
Little Rock

Memphis●
TENNESSEE
Chattanooga●
Tennessee

Columbia●
Atlanta●

Appalachian

Mountains

SOUTH CAROLINA

●Charleston

OKLAHOMA

Red

●Birmingham

GEORGIA
●Columbus

●Savannah

TEXAS
●Abilene

Fort Worth●●Dallas

●Monroe
Jackson★

MISSISSIPPI

ALABAMA

★Montgomery

●Jacksonville

LOUISIANA

FLORIDA
F★
Tallahassee

★Austin
●San Antonio

Baton Rouge★

●New Orleans

ATLANTIC
OCEAN

MEXICO

Rio Grande

Corpus Christi●

GULF OF MEXICO

Kilometres
0 100 200 300 400 500

Miles 0 100 200 300

●Orlando

●Cape
Canaveral

●Tampa

Fort Lauderdale●

●Miami

Left: Manhattan, the heart of
New York City, is an important
centre for business and trade.
There are many important
buildings in Manhattan such as
the United Nations and the
World Trade Center.

Gradually people with pioneering spirits ventured westwards and new states were formed. Some farmed on the mid-western plains while explorers and miners travelled through the Rocky Mountains all the way to the Pacific coast. Today people from all over the world live in the USA.

Like their Canadian neighbours, most Americans have a high standard of living. The USA is an extremely wealthy country. It has large resources of oil, gas, coal and many metals, huge farms and plantations and more factories than any other country in the world.

Above right: Las Vegas, Nevada is famous for gambling and nightclubs.

Right: This view of the Delaware River shows the rich growth and beauty of the New Jersey region.

Left: Oil drilling is a common sight in Texas.

Below: The government of the United States includes the Senate and the House of Representatives. They meet in the Capitol building in Washington D.C.

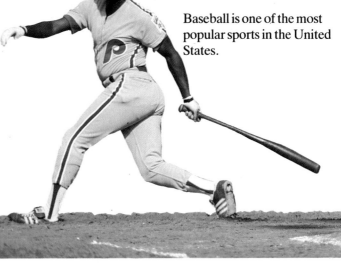

Baseball is one of the most popular sports in the United States.

Eastern and Southern States

State	Popular name	Capital	Bird	Flower	Tree
Alabama	Yellowhammer State	Montgomery	Yellowhammer	Camellia	Southern pine (Longleaf pine)
Arkansas	Land of Opportunity	Little Rock	Mockingbird	Apple blossom	Pine
Connecticut	Constitution State	Hartford	Robin	Mountain laurel	White oak
Delaware	First State	Dover	Blue hen chicken	Peach blossom	American holly
Florida	Sunshine State	Tallahassee	Mockingbird	Orange blossom	Cabbage palm
Georgia	Empire State of the South	Atlanta	Brown thrasher	Cherokee rose	Live oak
Kentucky	Bluegrass State	Frankfort	Kentucky cardinal	Goldenrod	Tulip poplar
Louisiana	Pelican State	Baton Rouge	Brown pelican	Magnolia	Bald cypress
Maine	Pine tree State	Augusta	Chickadee	White pine cone and tassel	White pine
Maryland	Old Line State	Annapolis	Baltimore oriole	Black-eyed Susan	White oak
Massachusetts	Bay State	Boston	Chickadee	Arbutus (Mayflower)	American elm
Mississippi	Magnolia State	Jackson	Mockingbird	Magnolia	Magnolia
New Hampshire	Granite State	Concord	Purple finch	Purple lilac	White birch
New Jersey	Garden State	Trenton	Eastern goldfinch	Purple violet	Red oak
New York	Empire State	Albany	Bluebird	Rose	Sugar maple
North Carolina	Tar Heel State	Raleigh	Cardinal	Flowering dogwood	Pine
Oklahoma	Sooner State	Oklahoma City	Scissor-tailed Flycatcher	Mistletoe	Redbud
Pennsylvania	Keystone State	Harrisburg	Ruffed grouse	Mountain laurel	Hemlock
Rhode Island	Little Rhody	Providence	Rhode Island Red	Violet	Red maple
South Carolina	Palmetto State	Columbia	Carolina wren	Carolina jessamine	Palmetto
Tennessee	Volunteer State	Nashville	Mockingbird	Iris	Tulip poplar
Texas	Lone Star State	Austin	Mockingbird	Bluebonnet	Pecan
Vermont	Green Mountain State	Montpelier	Hermit thrush	Red clover	Sugar maple
Virginia	Old Dominion	Richmond	Cardinal	Flowering dogwood	none
West Virginia	Mountain State	Charleston	Cardinal	Rhododendron	Sugar maple

This small church among trees turning colour is typical of the scenic Vermont countryside.

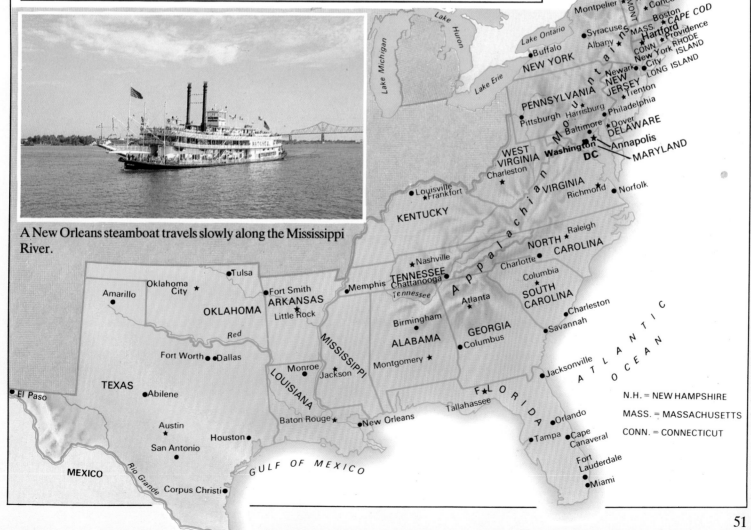

A New Orleans steamboat travels slowly along the Mississippi River.

N.H. = NEW HAMPSHIRE

MASS. = MASSACHUSETTS

CONN. = CONNECTICUT

The Midwest

State	Popular name	Capital	Bird	Flower	Tree
Illinois	Land of Lincoln	Springfield	Cardinal	Native Violet	White oak
Indiana	Hoosier State	Indianapolis	Cardinal	Peony	Tulip tree or Yellow poplar
Iowa	Hawkeye State	Des Moines	Eastern goldfinch	Wild rose	Oak
Kansas	Sunflower State	Topeka	Western meadow lark	Sunflower	Cottonwood
Michigan	Wolverine State	Lansing	Robin	Apple blossom	White pine
Minnesota	Gopher State	St Paul	Common loon	Pink and white lady's slipper	Norway or red pine
Missouri	Show Me State	Jefferson City	Bluebird	Hawthorn	Flowering dogwood
Nebraska	Cornhusker State	Lincoln	Western meadow lark	Goldenrod	American elm
North Dakota	Flickertail State	Bismarck	Western meadow lark	Wild prairie rose	American elm
Ohio	Buckeye State	Columbus	Cardinal	Scarlet carnation	Buckeye
South Dakota	Sunshine State	Pierre	Ring-necked pheasant	American pasque-flower	Black Hills spruce
Wisconsin	Badger State	Madison	Robin	Wood Violet	Sugar maple

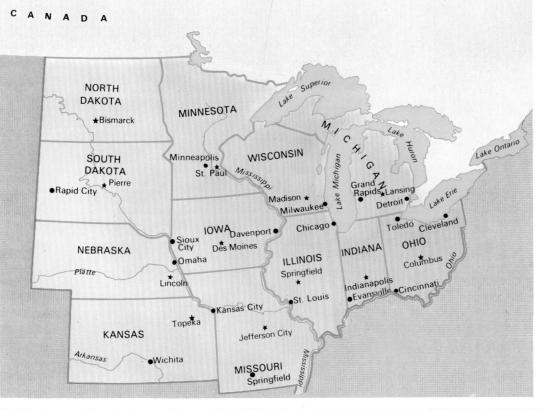

Automobile manufacturing is a very important industry in Detroit, Michigan. The industry provides jobs for many people. Car and truck parts are made and then they are assembled. This assembly line is at the Ford Motor Company.

Huge fields of soyabeans have been planted on this farm in Iowa. Most of the midwest is covered by farmland. Other important crops are corn, wheat, tobacco and maize. In addition, cattle, pigs and sheep are often raised.

Western and Mountain States

State	Popular name	Capital	Bird	Flower	Tree
Alaska	Last Frontier	Juneau	Willow ptarmigan	Forget-me-not	Sitka spruce
Arizona	Grand Canyon State	Phoenix	Cactus wren	Saguaro	Paloverde
California	Golden State	Sacramento	California valley quail	Golden poppy	California redwood
Colorado	Centennial State	Denver	Lark bunting	Rocky Mt. columbine	Blue spruce
Hawaii	Aloha State	Honolulu	Nene (Hawaiian goose)	Hibiscus	Kukui
Idaho	Gem State	Boise	Mountain bluebird	Syringa (Mock orange)	Western White pine
Montana	Treasure State	Helena	Western meadow lark	Bitterroot	Ponderosa pine
Nevada	Silver State	Carson City	Mountain bluebird	Sagebrush	Single-leaf piñon
New Mexico	Land of Enchantment	Santa Fe	Road runner	Yucca	Piñon or nut pine
Oregon	Beaver State	Salem	Western meadow lark	Oregon grape	Douglas fir
Utah	Beehive State	Salt Lake City	Seagull	Sego lily	Blue spruce
Washington	Evergreen State	Olympia	Willow goldfinch	Coast rhododendron	Western hemlock
Wyoming	Equality State	Cheyenne	Meadow lark	Indian paintbrush	Cottonwood

Right: You can meet Mickey Mouse and other Walt Disney characters in Disneyland. Disneyland is in California and Disneyworld is in Florida.

Cable cars run on tracks up and down the hilly streets of San Francisco.

For location of Alaska and Hawaii see (map) page 49.

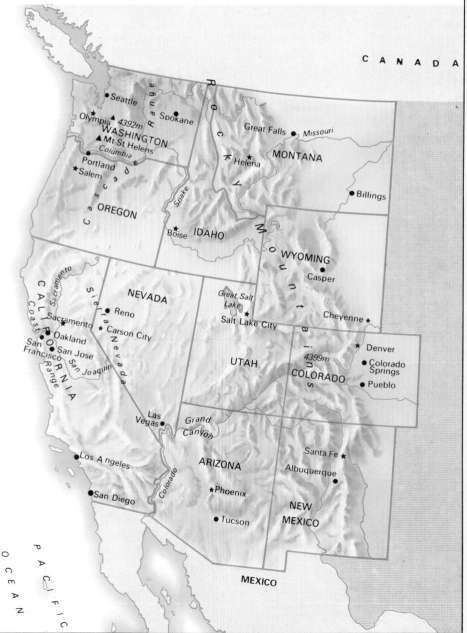

Mexico, the Caribbean,

Antigua & Barbuda

Bahamas

Barbados

Cuba

Dominica

Dominican Republic

Grenada

St Christopher Nevis

Haiti

Jamaica

St Lucia

St Vincent & Grenadines

Trinidad & Tobago

Mexico and seven small countries make up Central America – the land link between the United States and South America.

The people living in Central America and the islands of the West Indies are descendants either of the original people or of Europeans and Negroes. Most of them speak Spanish, English, French or American Indian languages. In 1492, when Christopher Columbus reached the islands in the Caribbean Sea, he thought he had sailed around the world to India. He called the people living there 'Indians' and the islands were named the West Indies.

Central America and the thousands of West Indian islands are mostly hot and mountainous. The climate is ideal for growing fruit, coffee, cotton, tobacco and sugar-cane. Cuba is the largest of the West Indian islands and it is the third largest producer of sugar in the world. Many of the islands are popular holiday places because of their sunny climate and easy-going atmosphere.

In Mexico most people work on small farms. The main crop is maize. A favourite meal is *tortillas*, a pancake made from maize flour. Gold and other metals are mined in Mexico, but the most important industry is oil.

Below left: The warm Caribbean Sea is ideal for sailing, swimming and snorkeling.

and Central America

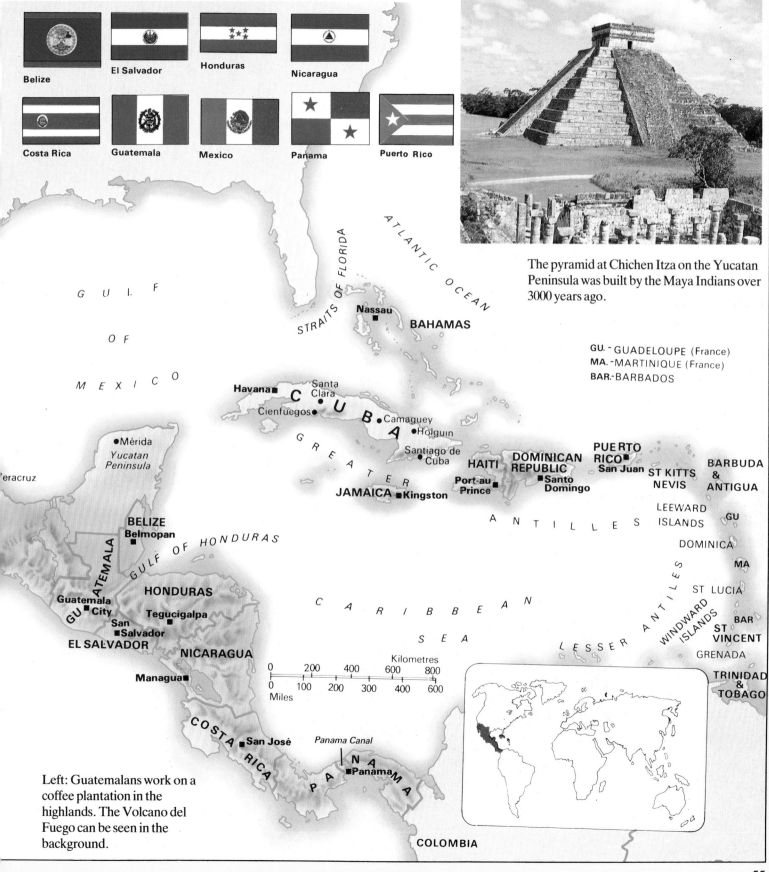

Belize

El Salvador

Honduras

Nicaragua

Costa Rica

Guatemala

Mexico

Panama

Puerto Rico

The pyramid at Chichen Itza on the Yucatan Peninsula was built by the Maya Indians over 3000 years ago.

GU. - GUADELOUPE (France)
MA. - MARTINIQUE (France)
BAR. - BARBADOS

ATLANTIC OCEAN

STRAITS OF FLORIDA

GULF OF MEXICO

Nassau

BAHAMAS

Havana
Santa Clara
Cienfuegos
CUBA
Camaguey
Holguin
Santiago de Cuba

GREATER

Mérida
Yucatan Peninsula

eracruz

HAITI
Port-au-Prince
JAMAICA
Kingston

DOMINICAN REPUBLIC
Santo Domingo

PUERTO RICO
San Juan

ST KITTS NEVIS

BARBUDA & ANTIGUA

LEEWARD ISLANDS

GU

DOMINICA

MA

BELIZE
Belmopan

GULF OF HONDURAS

GUATEMALA

Guatemala City

HONDURAS
Tegucigalpa

San Salvador
EL SALVADOR

NICARAGUA

Managua

ANTILLES

CARIBBEAN

SEA

LESSER ANTILLES

ST LUCIA

WINDWARD ISLANDS

BAR

ST VINCENT

GRENADA

TRINIDAD & TOBAGO

Kilometres
0   200   400   600   800
0 100   200   300   400   600
Miles

COSTA RICA
San José

Panama Canal

PANAMA
Panama

Left: Guatemalans work on a coffee plantation in the highlands. The Volcano del Fuego can be seen in the background.

COLOMBIA

The Andean Countries

The Andes mountains rise above much of Colombia, Ecuador, Peru and Bolivia. They form high tablelands or *plateaus* where the climate is cool even though the Equator passes through Ecuador and Colombia. Many rivers that feed the Amazon river begin in the Andes and travel eastwards through thick tropical forests.

Bananas and coffee are grown on plantations where the climate is hot and tropical. As transport across the mountains gets better, more people are living in the Amazon lowlands. Here they farm and work in mines. But much of the land is covered by thick forest and cannot be farmed.

Over 800 years ago the Andes were populated by the Incas. Gold and silver in the mountains attracted the Spaniards who eventually destroyed the Inca civilization. Today minerals are still important, especially in Bolivia. Spanish is the official language spoken in the Andean countries.

Colombia

Ecuador

Peru

Bolivia

Left: Llamas are herded in the Andes near Cuzco, Peru. Their wool is used to make warm clothing.

Below: Indians live in the interior of Colombia, far from the modern world. In this picture rice is pounded with a large mortar and pestles.

Above: Indians in colourful clothes gather in a market in Ecuador to sell their fruit and vegetables. Many Indians in the Andean countries still speak the old Indian languages Quechua and Aymara.

Below: Traditional reed boats lie on the beaches of Lake Titicaca in Peru. Some Peruvians make their living by fishing in the lake and farming the surrounding land.

PANAMA

Cartagena•
•Barranquilla
5775m▲

Medellin•
•Bucaramanga
VENEZUELA
GUYANA

Magdalena

■Bogotá

Cali•
▲
5750 m
COLOMBIA

Quito■
Guayaquil•
ECUADOR

Iquitos•
Amazon
BRAZIL

Piura•
Maranon

Chiclayo•
Trujillo•
Chimbote•
▲6768 m
Madeira

PERU
Beni

Callao•■Lima
•Huancayo

Cuzco•
▲6384 m
BOLIVIA

El Misti
5822m▲
Lake Titicaca
•La Paz

Arequipa•
Cochabamba•
•Santa Cruz

Lake Poopo
■Sucre

▲6755m

CHILE
PARAGUAY

PACIFIC
OCEAN

M o u n t a i n s
A n d e s

ARGENTINA

Kilometres
0   200   400   600   800
0 100 200 300 400 500
Miles

57

Brazil and its Neighbours

People of many different races live together in eastern South America. There are American Indians and *mestizos*, who are mixed Indian and European people. Other people are direct descendants of Europeans or Africans. Most of the early settlers were Spanish or Portuguese and most South Americans today speak one of these languages. Many people are also Roman Catholic.

Brazil is the largest country in South America. Much of the land is covered in thick Amazon rain forest. Most people live in big cities, such as Rio de Janeiro and São Paulo near the Atlantic coast. The north-eastern part of Brazil is poorer. Land is owned by a few rich landlords who employ farmers. In bad years the farmers have to go to the cities in search of other work.

Brazil is famous for growing coffee. Sugar cane is also an important crop. Coal, iron ore and other minerals are abundant in Brazil.

To the north-east of Brazil is Venezuela. Here rain forests also cover much of the land. Venezuela is a very rich country because it has valuable oil fields and iron ore. The money received from selling oil provides Venezuelans with factories, modern homes and roads.

Guyana, Surinam and French Guiana were once colonies of the British, Dutch and French. In these countries most people live in cities along the coast.

Above: The Amazon River flows through the thick, hot jungle. It is part of the world's greatest river system.

Left: The Indians living in the Mato Grosso region of Brazil often wear traditional face paint.

Right: A huge statue of Christ watches over Corcovado peak and the beautiful harbour of Rio de Janeiro. A lively carnival takes place in this city every year.

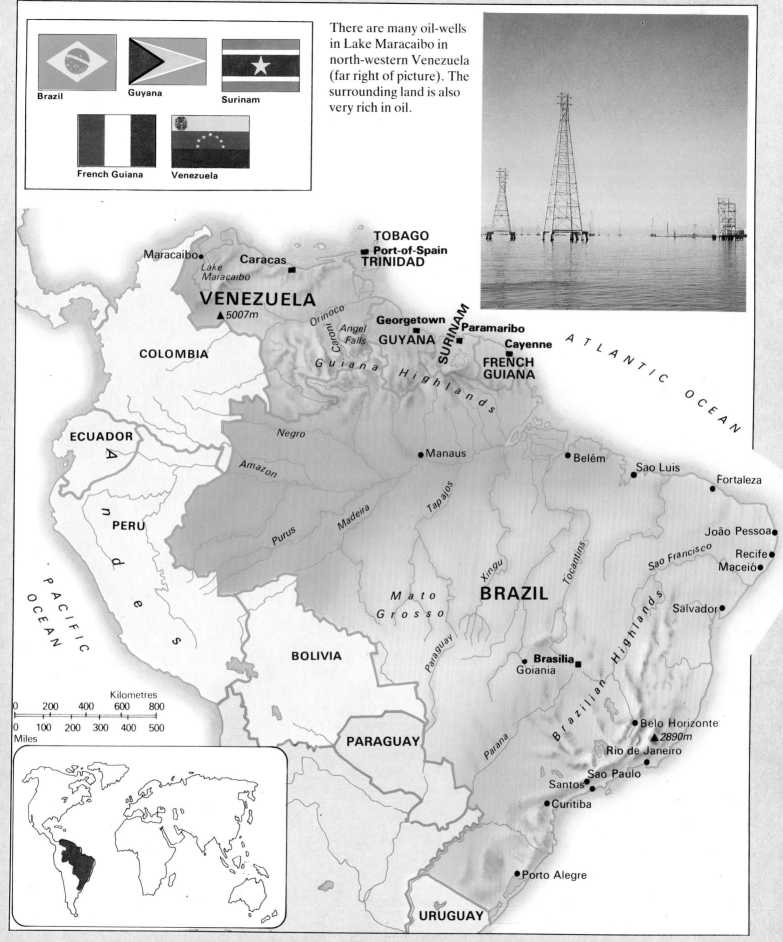

Brazil

Guyana

Surinam

French Guiana

Venezuela

There are many oil-wells in Lake Maracaibo in north-western Venezuela (far right of picture). The surrounding land is also very rich in oil.

MARACAIBO
Lake Maracaibo
Caracas
TOBAGO
Port-of-Spain
TRINIDAD
VENEZUELA
▲5007m
COLOMBIA
Orinoco
Caroni
Angel Falls
Georgetown
GUYANA
SURINAM
Paramaribo
Cayenne
FRENCH GUIANA
Guiana Highlands
ATLANTIC OCEAN
ECUADOR
Negro
Manaus
Belém
Sao Luis
Fortaleza
Amazon
Purus
Madeira
Tapajos
PERU
A n d e s
BOLIVIA
Xingu
Mato Grosso
Paraguay
Tocantins
Sao Francisco
João Pessoa
Recife
Maceió
BRAZIL
Salvador
Brazilian Highlands
Brasilia
Goiania
Belo Horizonte
▲2890m
Rio de Janeiro
PACIFIC OCEAN
Parana
PARAGUAY
Sao Paulo
Santos
Curitiba

Kilometres
0   200   400   600   800
0 100 200 300 400 500
Miles

Porto Alegre

URUGUAY

Southern South America

The countries of southern South America enjoy a mild climate, unlike their neighbours in the tropical north. The southern tip of the continent is very cool because it is not far from the frozen wastes of Antarctica.

Chile is long and narrow. In the north is the Atacama Desert where workers mine copper and nitrate. Many people in Chile try to live off the land, but farming is hard in most areas. People are leaving their farms to work in cities, such as Santiago and Valparaiso.

Argentina is the second largest and the richest of all South American countries. Farmers rear sheep and cattle, and grow wheat, sugar cane and cotton on the fertile *pampas* or grasslands. Factory workers in the cities process these products.

Most people living in Chile and Argentina are descendants of the Spanish and are Spanish speaking. People from Europe, especially from Italy are still going to live in these countries today.

Argentina

Chile

Paraguay

Uruguay

Above: Patagonia is the name of the upland plain in the south of Argentina. There are oil, coal and mineral deposits in this region.

Above left: Buenos Aires is the major port of Argentina.

Left: The copper mine at Chiquicamata in Chile is the largest open cast mine in the world.

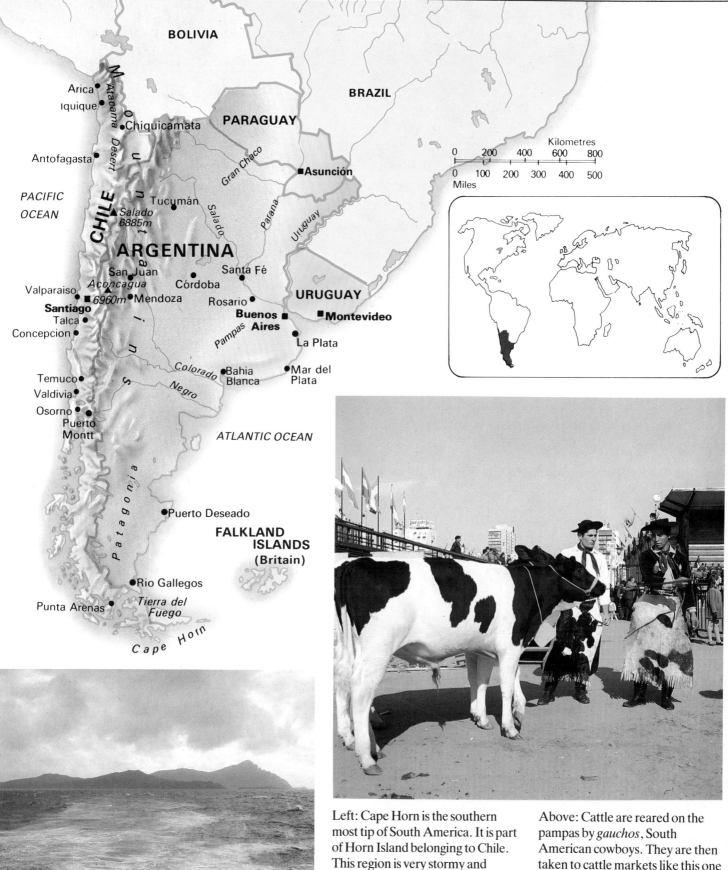

BOLIVIA

BRAZIL

PARAGUAY

Arica

Iquique

Chiquicamata

Antofagasta

Gran Chaco

■Asunción

PACIFIC
OCEAN

Tucumán

▲Salado
6885m

ARGENTINA

San Juan

Santa Fé

Aconcagua

Córdoba

Valparaiso

6960m

Mendoza

Rosario

Santiago

URUGUAY

Talca

Buenos
Aires

Montevideo

Concepcion

Pampas

La Plata

Colorado

Bahia
Blanca

Mar del
Plata

Temuco

Negro

Valdivia

ATLANTIC OCEAN

Osorno

Puerto
Montt

Patagonia

Puerto Deseado

FALKLAND
ISLANDS
(Britain)

Rio Gallegos

Punta Arenas

Tierra del
Fuego

Cape Horn

Kilometres
0 200 400 600 800

0 100 200 300 400 500
Miles

Left: Cape Horn is the southern
most tip of South America. It is part
of Horn Island belonging to Chile.
This region is very stormy and
dangerous for seamen to sail
around. Many ships go through the
Panama Canal instead.

Above: Cattle are reared on the
pampas by *gauchos*, South
American cowboys. They are then
taken to cattle markets like this one
in Mendoza, Argentina. Beef is one
of the country's most important
exports.

North Africa

The vast Sahara Desert covers almost all of northern Africa. It is the largest, hottest desert in the world, stretching for 4800 kilometres from the Atlantic Ocean to the Red Sea. In the north-west, in Morocco and Algeria, lie the rugged Atlas Mountains.

The people of northern Africa are mostly Muslim Arabs and Berbers who earn their living from farming. They live in river valleys and around oases, because there is no water in other areas. In Egypt it scarcely ever rains, except along the Mediterranean coast. Most farmers rely on the river Nile for water. The Aswan Dam, built on the Nile, stores water for use during dry periods.

Tourists travel to Tunisia and Morocco to enjoy sunbathing on the beaches and wandering through the colourful bazaars. But many more tourists visit Egypt to see the pyramids at Giza – one of the seven wonders of the world.

Below: The pyramids at Giza were built to be the burial tombs for the Kings of Ancient Egypt.
Below right: In Mali, boats carry goods along the Niger River.
Far right: Flare stacks around a desert oil field in Libya.

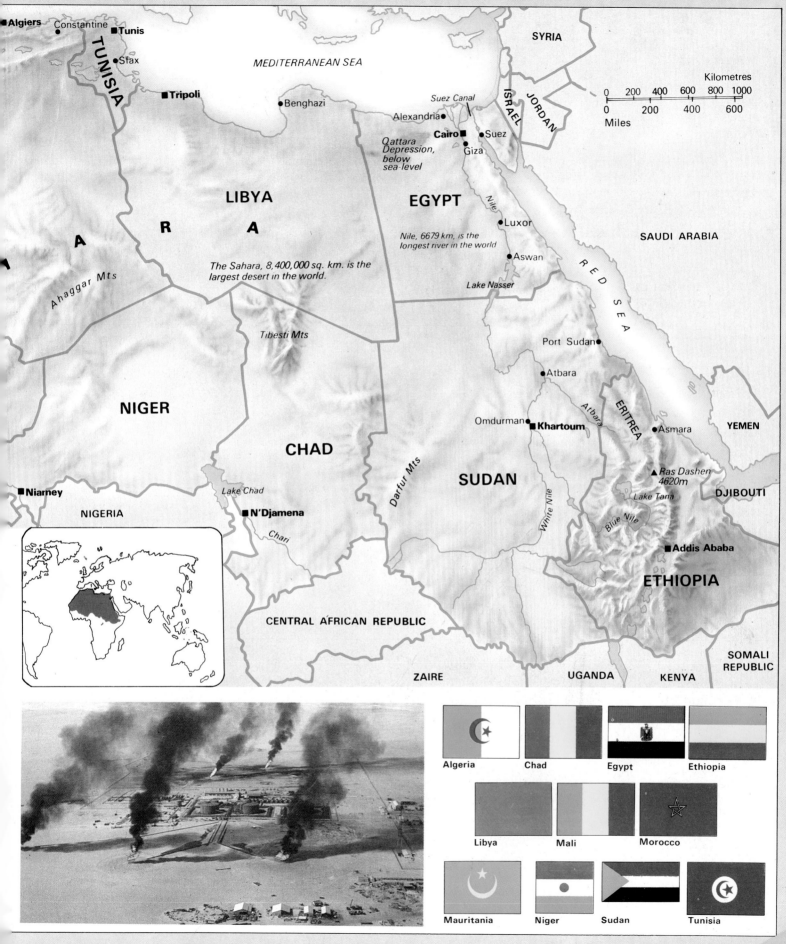

Algiers ● Constantine ● **Tunis**

TUNISIA

● Sfax

MEDITERRANEAN SEA

SYRIA

■ **Tripoli**

● Benghazi

Suez Canal

ISRAEL

JORDAN

Alexandria ●

Cairo ■ ● Suez

Qattara Depression, below sea-level

● Giza

A

R

A

LIBYA

EGYPT

Nile

● Luxor

SAUDI ARABIA

The Sahara, 8,400,000 sq. km. is the largest desert in the world.

Nile, 6679 km, is the longest river in the world

● Aswan

R E D

Ahaggar Mts

Lake Nasser

Tibesti Mts

S E A

● Port Sudan

NIGER

● Atbara

Atbara

ERITREA

YEMEN

Omdurman ● **Khartoum**

● Asmara

CHAD

SUDAN

▲ *Ras Dashen 4620m*

DJIBOUTI

Lake Chad

Darfur Mts

Lake Tana

Niamey

White Nile

Blue Nile

NIGERIA

■ **N'Djamena**

■ **Addis Ababa**

Chari

ETHIOPIA

CENTRAL AFRICAN REPUBLIC

ZAIRE

UGANDA

KENYA

SOMALI REPUBLIC

Kilometres
0 200 400 600 800 1000
0 200 400 600
Miles

Algeria	Chad	Egypt	Ethiopia
Libya	Mali	Morocco	
Mauritania	Niger	Sudan	Tunisia

West Africa

West Africa is a jigsaw puzzle of countries. Many different groups of Black Africans live there. Nigeria alone has 250 groups. The people speak a number of African languages including Swahili. But official languages are often English, French or Portuguese because most of these countries were once ruled by these European nations.

The countries along the coast are hot and have long, wet seasons. They are largely covered by tropical forest. Cocoa, coffee, palm oil and rubber are important crops. Root crops of cassava and yams provide food. Further inland, on savanna grasslands, crops consist of cotton and groundnuts. Millet, maize and sorghum are grown for food. Cattle are kept for their meat as well as for their hides and skins.

West African countries are building up their industries. There are new factories in Nigeria and Senegal, metals are mined in Sierra Leone and Ghana, and oil is drilled in Nigeria.

Crops and minerals are exported and the money received from selling these products is used to build modern towns, schools and hospitals. But many of the people still live on the land in the same way as their families have lived for centuries. Some live in clearings in the hot forests and work small gardens. Others herd animals on the *savanna* grasslands.

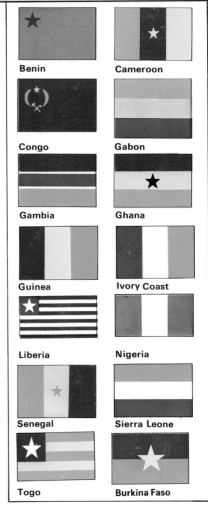

Benin · Cameroon · Congo · Gabon · Gambia · Ghana · Guinea · Ivory Coast · Liberia · Nigeria · Senegal · Sierra Leone · Togo · Burkina Faso

Left: A Nigerian woman in colourful dress stands in the centre of Lagos, the modern capital of Nigeria.

Below: Cocoa trees grow on large plantations in Ghana. Their huge pods are cut off with large knives. The beans inside are then dried and used to make chocolate and cocoa.

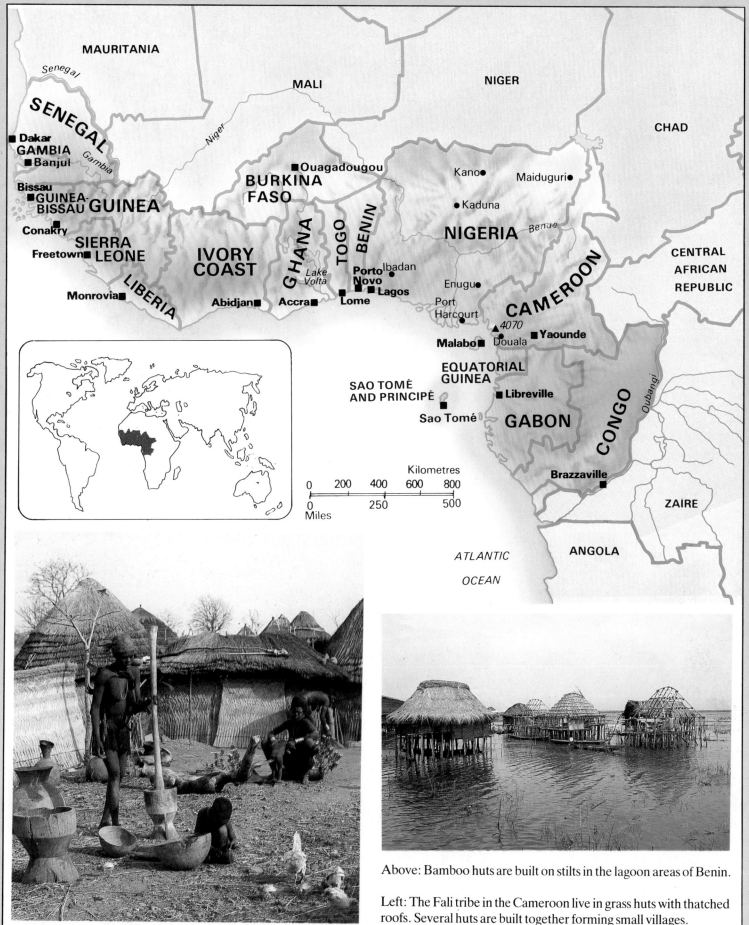

MAURITANIA

MALI

NIGER

CHAD

Senegal

SENEGAL

■ Dakar
GAMBIA
■ Banjul

Niger

Gambia

Bissau
■ GUINEA-
BISSAU   GUINEA

BURKINA
FASO

■ Ouagadougou

Kano●

Maiduguri●

● Kaduna

Conakry ■

SIERRA
LEONE

Freetown ■

IVORY
COAST

GHANA

TOGO

BENIN

NIGERIA

Benue

CENTRAL
AFRICAN
REPUBLIC

Monrovia ■

LIBERIA

Abidjan ■

*Lake
Volta*

Accra ■

Porto ■
Novo
Lome

Ibadan●
Lagos

Enugu●

Port ●
Harcourt

CAMEROON

▲ 4070

Malabo ■

Douala ■

■ Yaounde

SAO TOMÉ
AND PRINCIPÉ

EQUATORIAL
GUINEA

■ Libreville

Oubangui

Sao Tomé ■

GABON

CONGO

Kilometres

0   200   400   600   800

0   250   500
Miles

Brazzaville ■

ZAIRE

ATLANTIC

OCEAN

ANGOLA

Above: Bamboo huts are built on stilts in the lagoon areas of Benin.

Left: The Fali tribe in the Cameroon live in grass huts with thatched roofs. Several huts are built together forming small villages.

65

Central and East Africa

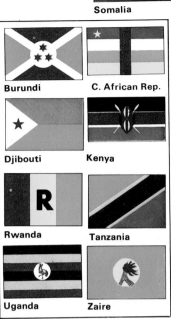

Somalia

Burundi
C. African Rep.
Djibouti
Kenya
Rwanda
Tanzania
Uganda
Zaire

Much of Central Africa is lowland covered with thick tropical forest. One of the greatest rivers in Africa, the river Zaire, runs through the region and is important for transport. Most people in Central Africa live in small clearings growing food crops such as yams and cassava. Sometimes parts of the forest are cleared for timber. Cocoa, coffee, palm oil and rubber are also important. Zaire's main source of wealth comes from copper mines in the south-eastern part of the country.

East Africa is a region of highland and *savanna* grassland. A cool climate is typical of the East African plateau. In the past Europeans settled in this area growing tea, coffee, cotton and sisal. Food crops consist of millet, maize and plantains.

Tourists often travel to Kenya to see wild animals. Once hunted, many lions, elephants, zebras and rhinos now live on large game reserves.

Somalia and Djibouti are mostly desert. The people living in these countries are animal herders and are often very poor.

The Bambuti, a tribe of pygmies, live in the forests of Zaire. They are the world's smallest people. They hunt game with spears, bows and arrows and fish with nets.

An elephant herd grazes on the grasslands of Kenya. Behind them is Mount Kilimanjaro, the highest peak in Africa.

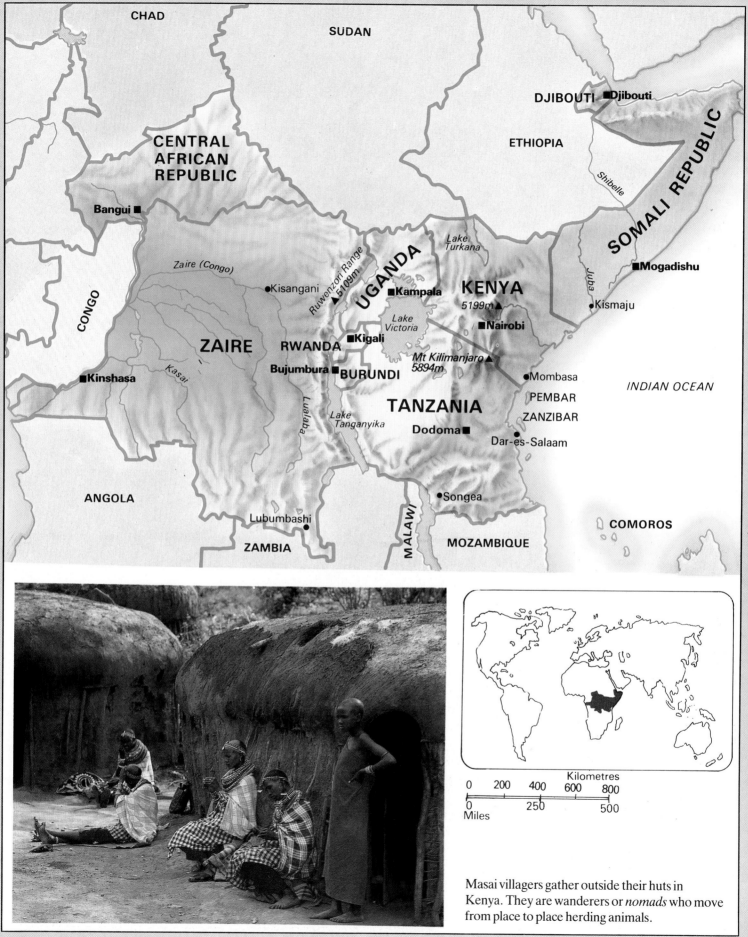

CHAD

SUDAN

CENTRAL
AFRICAN
REPUBLIC

DJIBOUTI ■Djibouti

ETHIOPIA

SOMALI REPUBLIC

Bangui ■

Shibelle

Zaire (Congo)

Lake
Turkana

CONGO

Kisangani ●

Ruwenzori Range
5109m ▲

UGANDA

■Kampala

KENYA

5199m ▲

Juba

■Mogadishu

●Kismaju

ZAIRE

RWANDA

Lake
Victoria

/ ■Nairobi

Kasai

■Kigali

Kinshasa ■

Bujumbura ■ BURUNDI

Mt Kilimanjaro ▲
5894m

●Mombasa

INDIAN OCEAN

Lualaba

TANZANIA

PEMBAR

ZANZIBAR

Lake
Tanganyika

Dodoma ■

●Dar-es-Salaam

ANGOLA

●Songea

COMOROS

Lubumbashi ●

MALAWI

MOZAMBIQUE

ZAMBIA

Kilometres

0   200   400   600   800

0   250   500
Miles

Masai villagers gather outside their huts in
Kenya. They are wanderers or *nomads* who move
from place to place herding animals.

Southern Africa

Southern Africa is very different from the rest of Africa. To start with its climate is cooler than the rest of Africa. Look for the Namib and Kalahari deserts on the map. Unlike the almost barren Sahara in northern Africa, the Kalahari is a dry, bush-covered plateau.

Many Europeans also live in this part of Africa. Large numbers of them first arrived in South Africa during the 1880s, attracted by the discovery of gold. Many stayed to farm the land or run mines and businesses.

South Africa and Zimbabwe are the richest countries in southern Africa. People from poorer countries, such as Botswana and Lesotho, often go to work in their large manufacturing industries. South Africa produces a huge share of the world's gold and diamonds. In Zimbabwe, there are large cattle ranches as well as maize, cotton, and tobacco farms.

In South Africa there is a government policy called *apartheid* to keep Europeans and Black Africans apart. Europeans control the government and own the major businesses. Madagascar is one of the largest islands in the world. Most people are farmers.

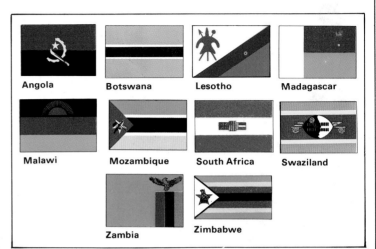

Angola   Botswana   Lesotho   Madagascar

Malawi   Mozambique   South Africa   Swaziland

Zambia   Zimbabwe

Above: Lake Kariba is on the border of Zimbabwe and Zambia. The Kariba dam in Zimbabwe provides water for the dry season.

Left: Gold is found in rock called ore. The ore is heated to melt the gold. This man is pouring gold into ingots.

Right: A Zulu woman wears her festival head-dress. The Zulus are the largest group of Black Africans in South Africa.

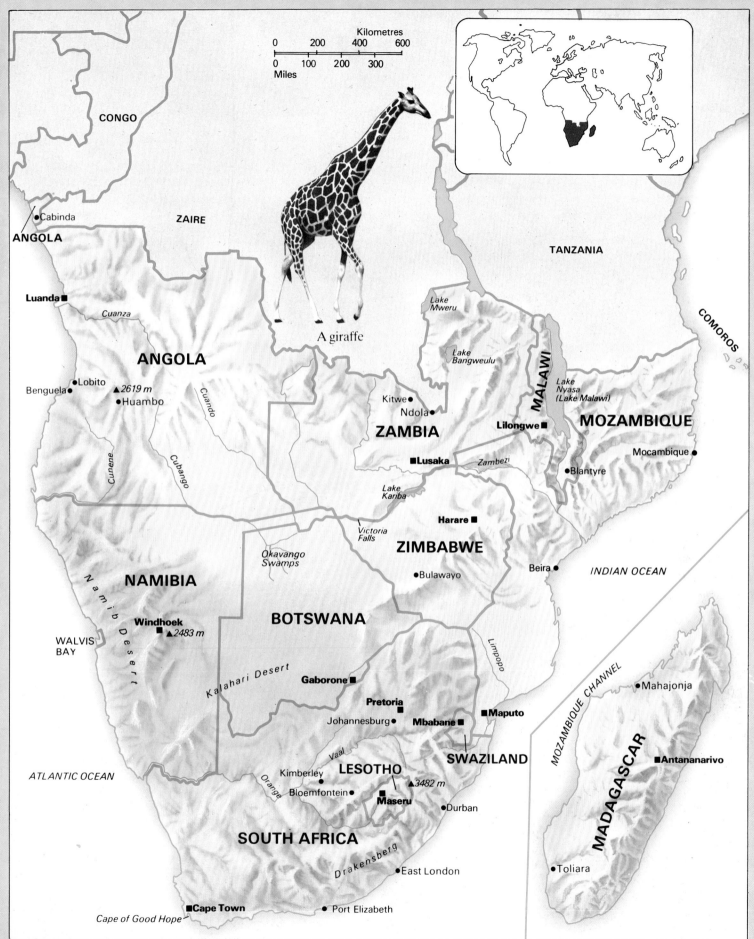

Kilometres
0   200   400   600

0   100   200   300
Miles

CONGO

ZAIRE

ANGOLA
•Cabinda

Luanda■

Cuanza

ANGOLA

Benguela• •Lobito
▲2619 m
•Huambo

Cuando

Cubango

Cunene

A giraffe

TANZANIA

Lake
Mweru

Lake
Bangweulu

Kitwe•
•Ndola
ZAMBIA

MALAWI

Lake
Nyasa
(Lake Malawi)

Lilongwe■

MOZAMBIQUE

Mocambique•

Lusaka■   *Zambezi*   •Blantyre

Lake
Kariba

Harare■

Victoria
Falls

ZIMBABWE

Okavango
Swamps

NAMIBIA

N a m i b   D e s e r t

Windhoek■ ▲2483 m

WALVIS
BAY

BOTSWANA

•Bulawayo

Beira•

INDIAN OCEAN

Limpopo

Kalahari Desert

Gaborone■

Pretoria■

Johannesburg•

Mbabane■   Maputo■

SWAZILAND

MOZAMBIQUE CHANNEL

•Mahajonja

MADAGASCAR

■Antananarivo

ATLANTIC OCEAN

Vaal

Kimberley•

Orange

Bloemfontein•

LESOTHO
▲3482 m

■
Maseru

•Durban

SOUTH AFRICA

Drakensberg

•Toliara

•East London

■Cape Town
Cape of Good Hope

•Port Elizabeth

COMOROS

69

Australia

Australia is the largest island and smallest continent in the world. It is sometimes called 'Down Under' because it lies south of the Equator among a group of islands in the Indian and Pacific Oceans.

Australia was discovered by Dutch sailors in the early 1600s. Much later in 1770, Captain Cook took possession of parts of eastern Australia for Britain. At that time the Aborigines were the only people living there. Later, in the 1850s gold was discovered and large numbers of settlers arrived from Europe in a hurry to make their fortunes. Today, besides gold, there are silver, copper, iron, zinc and aluminium mines.

Much of the west of Australia is desert. Although it is a big country it is not very crowded. Most people live in cities along the cooler south-east coast. In the dry, central plains called the 'Outback', there are sheep and cattle stations. Sheep are kept mainly for their wool which is sold to several other countries.

The Sydney Opera House was built to look like the sailboats in the harbour. Sydney is the largest city in Australia.

A koala

Left: Ayers Rock rises high above the flat desert in the Northern Territory.

Below: Sheep stations cover much of the land west of the Great Dividing Range. These merino sheep are raised for their wool.

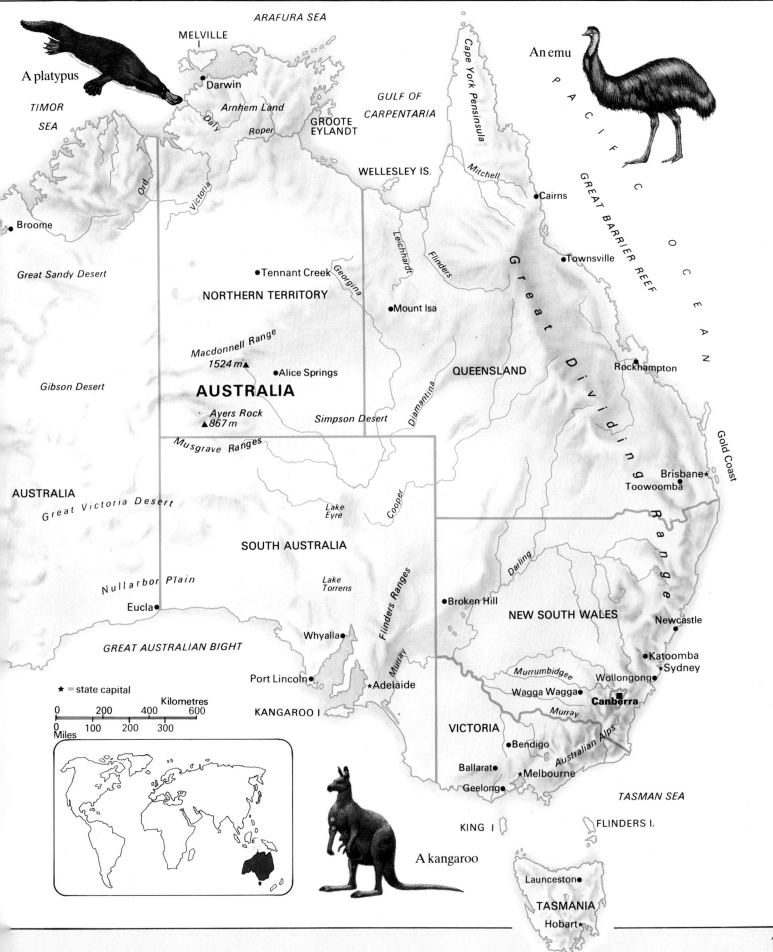

A platypus

ARAFURA SEA

MELVILLE I.

An emu

TIMOR SEA

• Darwin

Arnhem Land

Roper

GROOTE EYLANDT

GULF OF CARPENTARIA

Daly

Cape York Pensinsula

Mitchell

WELLESLEY IS.

PACIFIC

• Broome

Ord

Victoria

• Cairns

GREAT BARRIER REEF

Great Sandy Desert

Leichhardt

Georgina

Flinders

• Townsville

• Tennant Creek

NORTHERN TERRITORY

• Mount Isa

Gibson Desert

Macdonnell Range
1524 m▲

QUEENSLAND

Great Dividing

• Rockhampton

OCEAN

• Alice Springs

AUSTRALIA

Diamantina

▲ Ayers Rock
▲867 m

Simpson Desert

Musgrave Ranges

AUSTRALIA

Great Victoria Desert

Lake Eyre

Cooper

Gold Coast

• Brisbane ★
• Toowoomba

SOUTH AUSTRALIA

Darling

Range

Lake Torrens

Nullarbor Plain

Flinders Ranges

• Broken Hill

NEW SOUTH WALES

• Newcastle

Eucla •

GREAT AUSTRALIAN BIGHT

Whyalla •

Murray

• Katoomba
★ Sydney

Murrumbidgee

Wollongong •

Port Lincoln •

★ Adelaide

Wagga Wagga •

Canberra ■

★ = state capital

Kilometres
0   200   400   600
0   100   200   300
Miles

KANGAROO I

Murray

VICTORIA

Australian Alps

• Bendigo

Ballarat •
★ Melbourne

TASMAN SEA

A kangaroo

Geelong •

KING I

FLINDERS I.

Launceston •

TASMANIA

Hobart ★

New Zealand and the Pacific

New Zealand and the islands of the Pacific Ocean are divided into three groups – Melanesia, Micronesia and Polynesia – according to the type of people who live on the islands. Kiribati and the Caroline islands form part of Micronesia, but Fiji and Papua New Guinea are included in Melanesia.

New Zealand is part of Polynesia because the Maoris, the original inhabitants, are Polynesian people. New Zealand has two main islands, North Island and South Island. In the 1800s, settlers arrived from Britain to farm and to prospect for gold. Today most people live in towns and cities, and the largest city is Auckland. But New Zealand remains a rich farming country. Dairy farming is very important and there are over 9 million cattle and 55 million sheep. Many factory workers process meat, butter, cheese and milk.

Life on the Pacific Islands is often relaxed and simple. Many islanders live in small villages. They grow food in gardens and fish skilfully from canoes. Others on larger islands work on banana, coconut and cocoa plantations. Few islands have mineral resources, but phosphates are mined on Nauru and there are copper mines on Bougainville, one of the tiny islands that belongs to Papua New Guinea.

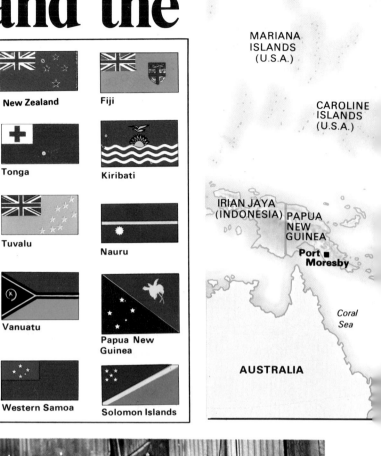

New Zealand — Fiji — Tonga — Kiribati — Tuvalu — Nauru — Vanuatu — Papua New Guinea — Western Samoa — Solomon Islands

MARIANA ISLANDS (U.S.A.)

CAROLINE ISLANDS (U.S.A.)

IRIAN JAYA (INDONESIA)

PAPUA NEW GUINEA

Port Moresby

Coral Sea

AUSTRALIA

Above: An experienced sheep shearer can clip the wool from a sheep in less than thirty seconds.

Left: The island of Bora Bora in the Pacific is one of the Society Islands belonging to France. It was made by volcanoes and is mountainous. Other islands nearby are flat and made of coral.

MEXICO

WAKE ISLAND
(U.S.A.)

Honolulu

HAWAII
(U.S.A.)

JOHNSTON ISLANDS
(U.S.A.)

REVILLA GIGEDO ISLANDS
(MEXICO)

MARSHALL ISLANDS
(U.S.A.)

CLIPPERTON ISLANDS
(FRANCE)

PALMYRA ISLANDS
(U.S.A.)
CHRISTMAS
ISLAND

THE PACIFIC

KIRIBATI
REPUBLIC

NAURU

GALAPAGOS
ISLANDS
(ECUADOR)

TUVALU

PHOENIX
ISLANDS

SOLOMON
ISLANDS

AMERICAN
SAMOA

MARQUESAS ISLANDS
(FRANCE)

PACIFIC

OCEAN

WESTERN
SAMOA

TUAMOTU ISLANDS
(FRANCE)

VANUATU
REPUBLIC

FIJI

Kilometres

0 200 400 600 800

COOK
ISLANDS
(NEW
ZEALAND)

SOCIETY
ISLANDS
(FRANCE)

NEW
CALEDONIA
(FRANCE)

TONGA

0   200   400
Miles

KERMADEC ISLANDS
(NEW ZEALAND)

PITCAIRN ISLAND
(BRITAIN)

EASTER ISLAND
(CHILE)

Kaitaia

Auckland

Hamilton

Rotorua

Gisborne

Lake
Taupo

New
Plymouth

Egmont
▲ 2516 m

Napier

NORTH
ISLAND

N
E
W

Z
E
A
L
A
N
D

TASMAN
SEA

Wanganui

Palmerston
North

Nelson

■ Wellington
Blenheim

Greymouth

The Kiwi is the
national bird of
New Zealand.

PACIFIC

OCEAN

Cook ▲
3764 m

Southern Alps

Christchurch

Timaru

SOUTH
ISLAND

Kilometres

0   100   200   300   400

0   50   100   150   200   250
Miles

Dunedin

Invercargill

There are hundreds of ancient stone
sculptures on Easter Island.
Archaeologists are still trying to discover
who made them. Polynesians live on
Easter Island today.

STEWART
ISLAND

73

The Polar Lands

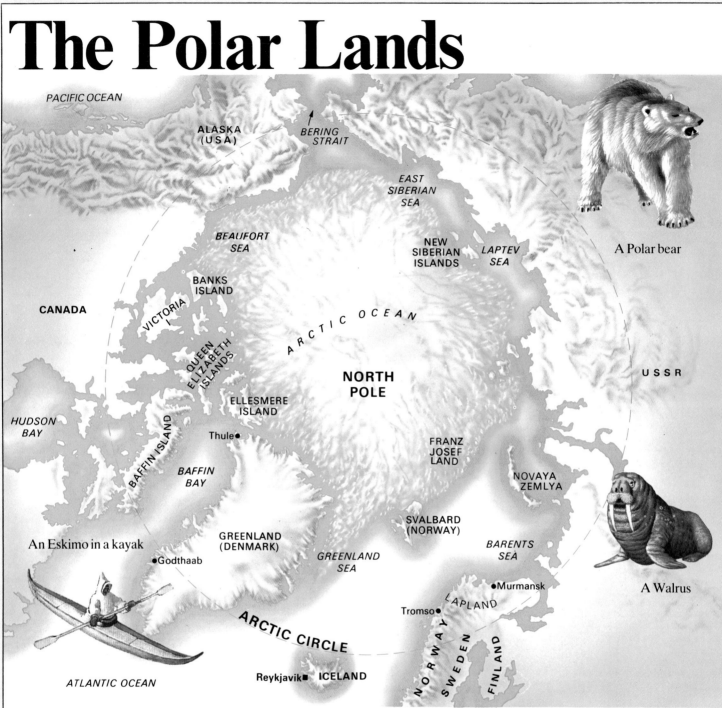

PACIFIC OCEAN

ALASKA
(USA)

BERING
STRAIT

EAST
SIBERIAN
SEA

BEAUFORT
SEA

NEW
SIBERIAN
ISLANDS

LAPTEV
SEA

BANKS
ISLAND

CANADA

VICTORIA
I.

ARCTIC OCEAN

QUEEN
ELIZABETH
ISLANDS

NORTH
POLE

USSR

ELLESMERE
ISLAND

HUDSON
BAY

Thule●

FRANZ
JOSEF
LAND

BAFFIN ISLAND

BAFFIN
BAY

NOVAYA
ZEMLYA

SVALBARD
(NORWAY)

An Eskimo in a kayak

GREENLAND
(DENMARK)

BARENTS
SEA

GREENLAND
SEA

●Godthaab

●Murmansk

LAPLAND

Tromso●

ATLANTIC OCEAN

ARCTIC CIRCLE

NORWAY

SWEDEN

FINLAND

Reykjavik■ ICELAND

A Polar bear

A Walrus

The Arctic

The area around the North Pole is called the Arctic. Much of it consists of the icy Arctic Ocean. But there are islands, including Greenland. Parts of North America, Europe and Asia also stretch beyond the *Arctic Circle*. The waters around the North Pole are frozen all the year round. But in other parts of the Arctic, the snow melts during the short summer weeks and patches of moss, lichen and bright flowers appear. These areas are the Arctic *tundra*. Eskimos are the only people living in the Arctic. Most live on the south-west coast of Greenland and are skilled hunters and fishermen.

The Antarctic

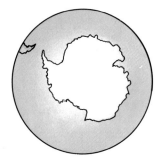

The continent of Antarctica covers more than 13 million square kilometres. It is larger than Europe and contains over 90 per cent of the world's ice and snow. It is so bitterly cold in Antarctica that no one has ever lived there permanently. Whalers went there in the 19th century, but they never left the safety of their ships. Since 1911, when the South Pole was reached for the first time by Roald Amundsen, many scientists have been to the continent. They study the weather and the structure of the rocks buried in the ice. Research stations have been built there by a few countries, including the USA and USSR.

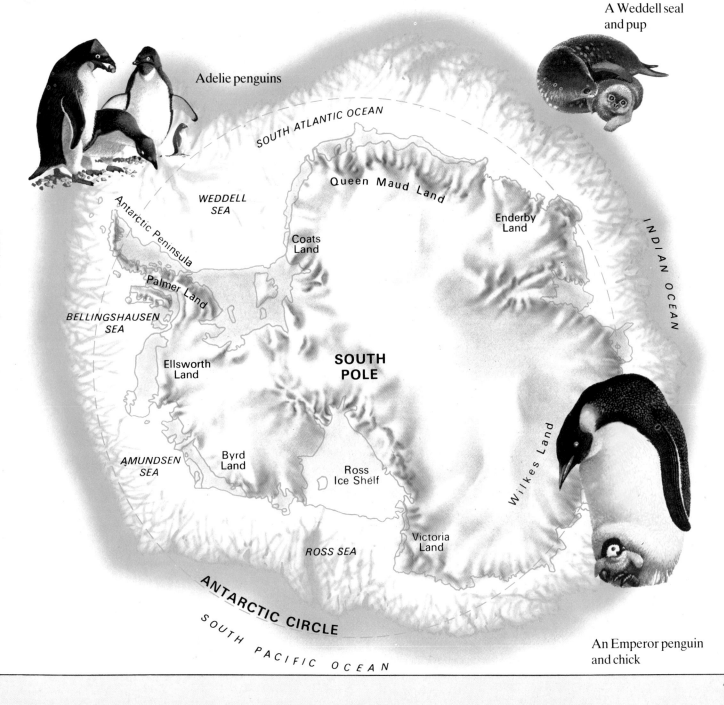

A Weddell seal and pup

Adelie penguins

SOUTH ATLANTIC OCEAN

Queen Maud Land

WEDDELL SEA

Enderby Land

Antarctic Peninsula

Coats Land

Palmer Land

INDIAN OCEAN

BELLINGSHAUSEN SEA

Ellsworth Land

SOUTH POLE

AMUNDSEN SEA

Byrd Land

Ross Ice Shelf

Wilkes Land

Victoria Land

ROSS SEA

ANTARCTIC CIRCLE

SOUTH PACIFIC OCEAN

An Emperor penguin and chick

Facts and Figures: Europe

Country	Area (sq km)	Population	Capital	Official Language	Currency	Major Products
Albania	28,748	3,000,000	Tirana	Albanian	Lek	Oil, bitumen, metals (chrome, nickel, copper), tobacco, fruit and vegetables
Andorra	453	32,700	Andorra la Vella	Catalan	French franc and Spanish peseta	Tourism, postage stamps
Austria	83,849	7,500,000	Vienna	German	Schilling	Food, iron and steel, textiles, paper products, machinery
Belgium	30,513	9,900,000	Brussels	Flemish, French	Belgian franc	Chemicals, vehicles, machinery, iron, steel
Bulgaria	110,912	8,900,000	Sofia	Bulgarian	Lev	Metals, machinery, textiles, tobacco, food
Czechoslovakia	127,869	15,500,000	Prague	Czech, Slovak	Koruna	Fuels, machinery, other manufactured goods, raw materials
Denmark	45,069	5,100,000	Copenhagen	Danish	Krone	Animals, meat, dairy produce, eggs, machinery, metals and metal goods
Estonia	45,099	1,571,000	Tallinn	Estonian	Rouble	Textiles, shipbuilding, mining equipment
Finland	337,009	4,900,000	Helsinki	Finnish, Swedish	Markka	Wood and wood pulp, paper, paperboard, machinery
France	547,026	55,000,000	Paris	French	French franc	Cars, electrical equipment, wine, cereals, textiles, leather goods, chemicals, iron, steel
Germany	356,755	77,700,000	Berlin	German	Deutschmark	Manufactured goods, chemicals, consumer goods, engineering goods
Greece	131,944	10,100,000	Athens	Greek	Drachma	Manufactured goods, food, animals, wine, tobacco, chemicals
Hungary	93,030	10,800,000	Budapest	Hungarian	Forint	Transport equipment, electrical goods, bauxite, aluminium, food, wine
Iceland	103,000	200,000	Reykjavik	Icelandic	Krona	Fish products
Ireland, Republic of	70,283	3,600,000	Dublin	English, Irish	Irish pound (punt)	Meat and meat products, dairy products, beer, whiskey
Italy	301,252	57,400,000	Rome	Italian	Lira	Machinery, motor vehicles, iron and steel, textiles, footwear, plastics, fruit
Latvia	63,960	2,673,000	Riga	Latvian	Rouble	Electric railway cars, telephone exchanges

Country	Area (sq km)	Population	Capital	Official Language	Currency	Major Products
Liechtenstein	157	26,000	Vaduz	German	Swiss franc	Cotton yarn and material, screws, bolts, needles
Lithuania	10,592	3,682,000	Vilnius	Lithuanian	Rouble	Cattle, electric motors and appliances
Luxembourg	2,586	400,000	Luxembourg City	French, Luxemburgish (a German dialect)	Luxembourg franc	Iron and steel, chemicals, vehicles, machinery
Malta	316	400,000	Valletta	Maltese, English	Maltese pound	Food, manufactured goods, ship repairing, tourism
Monaco	1.9	25,000	Monaco	French	French franc	Tourism
Netherlands	40,844	14,500,000	Amsterdam; The Hague is the Seat of government	Dutch	Guilder	Oil, chemicals, food and animals, machinery
Norway	324,219	4,200,000	Oslo	Norwegian	Krone	Animal products, paper, metals, metal products, fish, oil
Poland	312,677	37,300,000	Warsaw	Polish	Zloty	Lignite, coal, coke, iron and steel, ships, textiles, food
Portugal	92,082 (including Azores and Madeira)	10,400,000	Lisbon	Portuguese	Escudo	Textiles, timber, cork, machinery, chemicals, wine, sardines
Romania	237,500	22,800,000	Bucharest	Romanian	Leu	Food, machinery, minerals, metals, oil, natural gas, chemicals
San Marino	61	21,000	San Marino	Italian	Italian lira	Wine, cereals, cattle, tourism, postage stamps
Spain	504,782	38,600,000	Madrid	Spanish	Peseta	Manufactures goods, chemicals, textiles, leather, fish, wine and fruit
Sweden	449,964	8,300,000	Stockholm	Swedish	Swedish krona	Timber and timber products, machinery, metals and metal products, cars
Switzerland	41,288	6,500,000	Bern	French, German, Italian	Swiss franc	Tourism, machinery, chemicals and pharmaceuticals, watches, food, textiles
United Kingdom	244,828	56,400,000	London	English	Sterling pound	Manufactured goods, electrical engineering, textiles, chemicals and plastics
USSR	22,402,200	278,000,000	Moscow	Russian	Rouble	Iron, steel, chemicals, timber, paper, textiles (cotton), food, consumer goods
Vatican City State	0.44	1,000	Vatican City	Italian, Latin	Italian lira	
Yugoslavia	255,804	23,100,000	Belgrade	Serbo-Croat, Slovene, Macedonian	Dinar	Machinery, electrical goods, transport equipment, chemicals

Asia
Facts and Figures

Country	Area (sq km)	Population	Capital	Official Language	Currency	Major Products
Afghanistan	647,497	14,700,000	Kabul	Pashtu, Dari	Afghani	Skins, cotton, natural gas, fruit
Bahrain	622	400,000	Manama	Arabic	Dinar	Oil
Bangladesh	143,998	101,500,000	Dhaka	Bengali	Taka	Jute, leather, hide and skins, tea
Bhutan	47,000	1,400,000	Thimphu	Dzongkha	Ngultrum	Rice, fruit, timber
Brunei	5,765	200,000	Bandar Seri Begawan	Malay	Brunei dollar	Oil
Burma (Myanmar)	676,552	36,900,000	Rangoon	Burmese	Kyat	Teak, oil cake, rubber, jute
Cambodia (Kampuchea)	181,035	6,200,000	Phnom Penh	Khmer	Riel	Rice, rubber
China	9,596,961	1,042,000,000	Beijing (Peking)	Chinese (Mandarin)	Yuan	Industrial and agricultural products
Cyprus	9,251	700,000	Nicosia	Greek, Turkish	Pound	Fruit, vegetables, wine, manufactured goods, minerals
Hong Kong	1,045	5,500,000	Victoria	English, Chinese (Cantonese)	Hong Kong dollar	Light manufactured goods, textiles, electronics
India	3,287,590	762,200,000	Delhi	Hindi, English	Rupee	Tea, industrial goods, jute, textiles
Indonesia	2,027,087	168,400,000	Jakarta	Bahasa (Indonesian)	Rupiah	Oil, palm products, rubber, coffee
Iran	1,648,000	45,100,000	Tehran	Persian (Farsi)	Rial	Oil, natural gas, cotton
Iraq	434,924	15,500,000	Baghdad	Arabic	Iraqi dinar	Oil, dates, wool, cotton
Israel	20,770	4,200,000	Jerusalem	Hebrew, Arabic	Shekel	Cut diamonds, chemicals, fruit, tobacco
Japan	372,313	120,800,000	Tokyo	Japanese	Yen	Optical equipment, ships, vehicles, machinery, electronic goods, chemicals, textiles
Jordan	97,740	3,600,000	Amman	Arabic	Jordanian dinar	Phosphates, fruit, vegetables

Country	Area (sq km)	Population	Capital	Official Language	Currency	Major Products
Korea, North	120,538	20,100,000	Pyongyang	Korean	Won	Iron and other metal ores
Korea, South	98,484	42,700,000	Seoul	Korean	Won	Textiles, manufactured goods, chemicals
Kuwait	17,818	1,900,000	Kuwait	Arabic	Kuwait dinar	Oil, chemicals
Laos	236,800	3,800,000	Vientiane	Lao	Kip	Timber, coffee
Lebanon	10,400	2,600,000	Beirut	Arabic	Lebanese pound	Precious metals, gemstones
Macao	16	300,000	Macao	Portuguese, Chinese	Pataca	Light manufactured goods
Malaysia	329,749	15,700,000	Kuala Lumpur	Malay	Malaysian dollar	Rubber, tin, palm oil, timber
Maldive Islands	298	200,000	Malé	Divehi	Rupee	Fish, copra
Mongolia	1,565,000	1,900,000	Ulan Bator	Mongol	Tugrik	Cattle, horses, wool, hair
Nepal	140,797	17,000,000	Katmandu	Nepali	Rupee	Grains, hides, cattle, timber
Oman	212,457	1,200,000	Muscat	Arabic	Omani riyal	Oil, dates, limes, tobacco, frankincense
Pakistan	803,943	99,200,000	Islamabad	Urdu	Rupee	Cotton, carpets, leather, rice
Philippines	300,000	56,800,000	Manila	English, Pilipino	Peso	Sugar, timber, coconut products
Qatar	11,000	300,000	Doha	Arabic	Qatar riyal	Oil
Saudi Arabia	2,149,690	11,200,000	Riyadh	Arabic	Riyal	Oil
Singapore	581	2,600,000	Singapore	Malay, Chinese, Tamil, English	Singapore dollar	Refined oil products, electronic goods, rubber
Sri Lanka	65,610	16,400,000	Colombo	Sinhala	Rupee	Tea, rubber, coconut products, industrial goods
Syria	71,504	10,600,000	Damascus	Arabic	Syrian pound	Cotton, oil, cereals, animals

Country	Area (sq km)	Population	Capital	Official Language	Currency	Major Products
Taiwan	35,961	19,200,000	Taipei	Chinese (Mandarin)	Taiwan dollar	Textiles, electrical goods, plastics, machinery, food
Thailand	514,000	52,700,000	Bangkok	Thai	Baht	Rice, tapioca, rubber, tin
Turkey	780,576	52,100,000	Ankara	Turkish	Turkish lira	Cotton, tobacco, nuts, fruit
United Arab Emirates	83,600	1,300,000	Abu Dhabi	Arabic	Dirham	Oil, natural gas
Vietnam	329,556	60,500,000	Hanoi	Vietnamese	Dong	Fish, coal, agricultural goods
Yemen	527,968	8,200,000	San'a	Arabic	Riyal	Cotton, coffee, hides and skins, fish, refined oil

North America
Facts and Figures

Country	Area (sq km)	Population	Capital	Official Language	Currency	Major Products
Antigua and Barbuda	442	100,000	St John's	English	East Caribbean dollar	Oil products
Bahamas	13,935	200,000	Nassau	English	Bahamian dollar	Oil products
Barbados	431	300,000	Bridgetown	English	East Caribbean dollar	Sugar, oil products, electrical goods, clothing
Belize	22,965	200,000	Belmopan	English, Spanish	Belize dollar	Sugar, bananas, citrus products, fish, clothing
Canada	9,976,130	25,400,000	Ottawa	English, French	Canadian dollar	Wheat, natural gas, oil, wood pulp, newsprint, iron ore, cars and parts, fish
Costa Rica	50,700	2,600,000	San José	Spanish	Colon	Coffee, bananas, manufactured goods
Cuba	114,524	10,100,000	Havana	Spanish	Peso	Sugar, tobacco

Country	Area (sq km)	Population	Capital	Official Language	Currency	Major Products
Dominica	751	100,000	Roseau	English	East Caribbean dollar	Citrus fruits, bananas
Dominican Republic	48,734	6,200,000	Santo Domingo	Spanish	Peso	Sugar, coffee
El Salvador	21,041	5,100,000	San Salvador	Spanish	Colon	Coffee, cotton
Grenada	344	100,000	St George's	English	East Caribbean dollar	Cocoa, nutmeg, mace, bananas
Guatemala	108,889	8,000,000	Guatemala City	Spanish	Quetzal	Coffee, bananas, cotton, beef
Haiti	27,750	5,800,000	Port-au-Prince	French	Gourde	Coffee, bauxite, sugar
Honduras	112,088	4,400,000	Tegucigalpa	Spanish	Lempira	Coffee, bananas, timber, meat
Jamaica	10,991	2,300,000	Kingston	English	Jamaican dollar	Bauxite, alumina
Mexico	1,972,547	79,700,000	Mexico City	Spanish	Peso	Oil, coffee, cotton, sugar, manufactured goods
Nicaragua	130,000	3,000,000	Managua	Spanish	Cordoba	Cotton, coffee, meat, chemicals
Panama	75,650	2,000,000	Panama	Spanish	Balboa	Bananas, shrimps, sugar, oil products
St Christopher (St Kitts) and Nevis	262	40,000	Basseterre	English	East Caribbean dollar	Sugar
St Lucia	616	100,000	Castries	English	East Caribbean dollar	Bananas, cocoa, citrus fruits, coconuts, tourism, manufactured goods
St Vincent and the Grenadines	388	100,000	Kingstown	English	East Caribbean dollar	Bananas, arrowroot, coconuts
Trinidad and Tobago	5,130	1,200,000	Port of Spain	English	Trinidad dollar	Oil, asphalt, chemicals, sugar, fruit, cocoa, coffee
United States	9,363,123	238,900,000	Washington DC	English	US Dollar	Machinery, vehicles, aircraft and parts, iron and steel goods, coal, chemicals, cereals, soya beans, textiles, cotton

South America

Facts and Figures

Country	Area (sq km)	Population	Capital	Official Language	Currency	Major Products
Argentina	2,766,889	30,600,000	Buenos Aires	Spanish	Peso	Meat and meat products, tobacco, textiles, leather, machinery
Bolivia	1,093,581	6,200,000	La Paz (Seat of government); Sucre (Legal capital)	Spanish	Peso	Tin, oil, natural gas, cotton
Brazil	8,511,965	138,400,000	Brasilia	Portuguese	Cruzeiro	Machinery, vehicles, soya beans, coffee, cocoa
Chile	765,945	12,000,000	Santiago	Spanish	Peso	Wood pulp, paper, copper, timber, iron ore, nitrates
Colombia	1,138,914	29,400,000	Bogota	Spanish	Peso	Coffee, emeralds, sugar, oil, meat, skins and hides
Ecuador	283,561	8,900,000	Quito	Spanish	Sucre	Oil, bananas, cocoa, coffee
French Guiana	91,000	76,000	Cayenne	French	French franc	Bauxite, shrimps, bananas
Guyana	214,000	800,000	Georgetown	English	Guyanese dollar	Sugar, rice, bauxite, alumina, timber
Paraguay	406,752	3,600,000	Asunción	Spanish	Guarani	Cotton, soya beans, tobacco, timber
Peru	1,285,216	19,500,000	Lima	Spanish	Sol	Metals, minerals (silver, lead, zinc, copper), fish
Surinam	163,265	400,000	Paramaribo	Dutch, English	Guilder	Bauxite, alumina, rice, citrus fruit
Uruguay	176,216	3,000,000	Montevideo	Spanish	Peso	Meat, wool, hides and skins
Venezuela	912,050	17,300,000	Caracas	Spanish	Bolivar	Oil, iron, cocoa, coffee

Africa
Facts and Figures

Country	Area (sq km)	Population	Capital	Official Language	Currency	Major Products
Algeria	2,381,741	22,200,000	Algiers	Arabic	Algerian dinar	Natural gas, oil
Angola	1,246,700	7,900,000	Luanda	Portuguese	Kwanza	Coffee, diamonds, oil
Benin	112,622	4,000,000	Porto Novo	French	Franc CFA	Cocoa, cotton
Botswana	600,372	1,100,000	Gaborone	English, Setswana	Pula	Copper, diamonds, meat
Burkina Faso	274,200	6,900,000	Ouagadougou	French	Franc CFA	Livestock, groundnuts, cotton
Burundi	27,834	4,600,000	Bujumbura	French, Kirundi	Burundi franc	Coffee
Cameroon	475,442	9,700,000	Yaoundé	English, French	Franc CFA	Cocoa, coffee, oil
Cape Verde Islands	4,033	300,000	Praia	Portuguese	Escudo	Bananas, fish
Central African Republic	622,984	2,700,000	Bangui	French	Franc CFA	Coffee, diamonds, timber
Chad	1,284,000	5,200,000	N'Djamena	French	Franc CFA	Cotton, cattle, meat
Comoros	2,171	500,000	Moroni	French	Franc CFA	Spices
Congo	342,000	1,700,000	Brazzaville	French	Franc CFA	Oil, timber
Djibouti	22,000	300,000	Djibouti	French	Djibouti franc	Cattle, hides and skins
Egypt	1,001,449	48,300,000	Cairo	Arabic	Egyptian pound	Cotton, oil, textiles
Equatorial Guinea	28,051	300,000	Malabo	Spanish	Ekuele	Cocoa, coffee, timber
Ethiopia	1,221,900	36,000,000	Addis Ababa	Amharic	Ethiopian dollar	Coffee, hides and skins

Country	Area (sq km)	Population	Capital	Official Language	Currency	Major Products
Gabon	267,667	1,000,000	Libreville	French	Franc CFA	Manganese, oil
Gambia	11,295	800,000	Banjul	English	Dalasi	Groundnuts
Ghana	238,537	14,300,000	Accra	English	Cedi	Cocoa, gold, timber
Guinea	245,957	6,100,000	Conakry	French	Syli	Alumina, bauxite
Guinea-Bissau	36,125	900,000	Bissau	Portuguese	Escudo	Fish, groundnuts
Ivory Coast	322,463	10,100,000	Abidjan	French	Franc CFA	Cocoa, coffee, timber
Kenya	582,646	20,200,000	Nairobi	English, Swahili	Kenya shilling	Coffee, tea, hides
Lesotho	30,355	1,500,000	Maseru	English, Sesotho	Loti	Wool, mohair
Liberia	111,369	2,200,000	Monrovia	English	Liberian dollar	Iron ore, rubber
Libya	1,759,540	4,000,000	Tripoli	Arabic	Libyan dinar	Oil
Madagascar	587,041	10,000,000	Antananarivo	French, Malagasy	Malgache franc	Coffee, spices, vanilla
Malawi	118,484	7,100,000	Lilongwe	English, Chichewa	Kwacha	Tobacco, tea
Mali	1,240,000	7,700,000	Bamako	French	Mali franc	Groundnuts, cotton
Mauritania	1,030,700	1,900,000	Nouakchott	Arabic, French	Ouguiya	Iron ore, copper
Mauritius	2,085	1,000,000	Port Louis	English	Rupee	Sugar, tea, tobacco
Morocco	446,550	24,300,000	Rabat	Arabic	Dirham	Phosphates, fruit
Mozambique	783,030	13,900,000	Maputo	Portuguese	Metical	Sugar, fruit, vegetables
Namibia	824,292	1,100,000	Windhoek	Afrikaans, English	Rand	Minerals, diamonds, fish

Country	Area (sq km)	Population	Capital	Official Language	Currency	Major Products
Niger	1,267,000	6,500,000	Niamey	French	Franc CFA	Groundnuts, livestock, uranium
Nigeria	923,768	91,200,000	Lagos	English	Naira	Oil, palm kernels, cocoa
Rwanda	26,338	6,300,000	Kigali	French, Kinyarwanda	Rwanda franc	Coffee
Sao Tomé and Principé	965	100,000	Sao Tomé	Portuguese	Dobra	Cocoa
Senegal	196,192	6,700,000	Dakar	French	Franc CFA	Groundnuts, phosphates
Seychelles	280	100,000	Victoria	English, French	Rupee	Copra, fish, spices
Sierra Leone	71,740	3,600,000	Freetown	English	Leone	Diamonds, iron ore
Somali Republic	637,657	6,500,000	Mogadishu	Somali	Somali shilling	Livestock
South Africa	1,221,037	32,500,000	Pretoria (Seat of government); Cape Town (Legal capital)	Afrikaans, English	Rand	Gold, diamonds, fruit, vegetables
Sudan	2,505,813	21,800,000	Khartoum	Arabic	Sudanese pound	Cotton, groundnuts
Swaziland	17,363	600,000	Mbabane	English	Lilangeni	Sugar, wood pulp, asbestos, fruit
Tanzania	945,087	21,700,000	Dodoma	English, Swahili	Tanzanian shilling	Coffee, cotton, sisal, spices
Togo	56,000	3,000,000	Lomé	French	Franc CFA	Phosphates, cocoa, coffee
Tunisia	163,610	7,200,000	Tunis	Arabic	Tunisian dinar	Phosphates, olive oil, oil
Uganda	236,036	14,700,000	Kampala	English	Ugandan shilling	Coffee, cotton
Zaire	2,345,409	33,100,000	Kinshasa	French	Zaire	Coffee, cobalt, copper
Zambia	752,614	6,800,000	Lusaka	English	Kwacha	Copper
Zimbabwe	390,580	8,600,000	Harare	English	Zimbabwe dollar	Tobacco

Oceania
Facts and Figures

Country	Area (sq km)	Population	Capital	Official Language	Currency	Major Products
Australia	7,686,849	15,800,000	Canberra	English	Australian dollar	Cereals, meat, sugar, honey, fruit, metals and mineral ores, wool
Fiji	18,274	700,000	Suva	English, Fijian	Fiji dollar	Sugar, coconut oil
Kiribati	931	60,000	Tarawa	English, Gilbertese	Australian dollar	Copra, phosphates, fish
Nauru	21	8,000	Nauru	English, Nauruan	Australian dollar	Phosphates
New Zealand	268,676	3,400,000	Wellington	English	New Zealand dollar	Meat, dairy products, wool, fruit
Papua New Guinea	461,691	3,300,000	Port Moresby	English	Kina	Copra, cocoa, coffee, copper
Solomon Islands	28,446	300,000	Honiara	English	Solomon Islands dollar	Timber, fish, copra, palm oil
Tonga	699	100,000	Nuku'alofa	English	Pa'anga	Copra, bananas
Tuvalu	25	8,000	Funafuti	English, Tuvalu	Australian dollar	Copra
Vanuatu	14,763	100,000	Port Vila	Bislama, English, French	Vatu	Copra, fish
Western Samoa	2,842	200,000	Apia	English, Samoan	Tala	Copra, cocoa, bananas

General Index

Map Index

PHOTOGRAPHIC ACKNOWLEDGEMENTS

The publishers wish to thank ZEFA for supplying the photographs for the cover and most of the photographs inside the book.

Additional photographs were supplied by J. Allan Cash (p. 9 *right*), Royal Netherlands Embassy (p. 17), British Tourist Board (p. 18 *top*), Renault (p. 20 *top right*), Italian Tourist Office (p. 28 *top*), Hungarian Tourist Office (p. 30 *bottom*), Greek Tourist Office (p. 33 *top*), Novosti (p. 34 *left*), Dave Collins (p. 38 *top right*), Sharp Electronics (p. 42 *top*), Thailand Tourist Board (p. 44 *top left*), New Jersey Travel and Tourism (p. 50 *right*), Rowntrees (p. 64 *right*), Satour (p. 68 *left* and *bottom*), Australian News and Information Bureau (p. 70 *left* and *top*), New Zealand Tourist Office (p. 72 *right*).